The Cookout Book

THE COOKOUT BOOK

*Selected Recipes from America's Cookout Championships,
with an introduction to the techniques of barbecue cooking
and entertaining by Helen Evans Brown & Philip S. Brown*

THE WARD RITCHIE PRESS

1961

Photography

GEORGE DE GENNARO, *with the exception of the frontispiece which was made at the 1959 Cookout in Honolulu*

Illustrations

HARRY O. DIAMOND

Editorial

MARKA RITCHIE

Contents

The Cookout Recipes

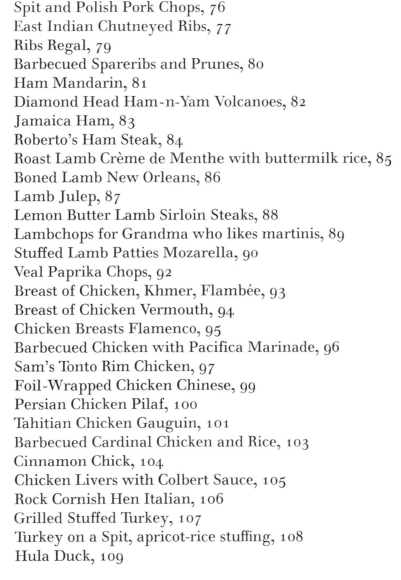

Introduction to Barbecue Cooking and Entertaining

Barbecue Cooking and Entertaining

THAT THE BEST COOKS, particularly outdoor cooks, are men, was dramatically proven during the first two Kaiser Cookouts, held in Hawaii in 1959 and 1960. Both times the 25 men finalists, competing for the title of "America's Cookout Champion of the Year," were noteworthy not only for their skill at the grill, but also for their personality, good humor, and obvious superiority. No conformists here! Like their recipes, the men themselves had distinction. All were individualists—some really characters, but charming ones—and all were well equipped with brains. But this figures, as professional men, executives, and intellectuals have often turned to one of the arts for a creative outlet. Now many have discovered The Art of Cookery. The Kaiser Cookouts, past and future, should stimulate this masculine interest and competitiveness and result, we hope and believe, in finer American cuisine.

The Kaiser Cookouts are for *men* only, and for them the rules were a cinch. They had to submit a complete recipe for an outdoor main dish, giving title, ingredients, and method of preparation; then mail it by a certain date. They had to be residents of the U.S.A. and 21 years of age or over, and of course they were supposed to give their names and addresses, an item that some of the potential prize-winners forgot. All entries without names, without proper postmark, or with other infringement of the rules were automatically jettisoned. Next came the second weeding, when unworkable recipes were discarded. Recipes that survived were barbecue-tested. Many didn't make that hurdle. Next came the task of picking the 25 best in the remaining batch. After blood, sweat, and cheers, the 25 finalists were chosen. These winners and their wives were given free, a trip to Hawaii, lodging at the fabulous Hawaiian Village, their fares, meals, tips, entertainment, and the gear used in their cooking, including the cookout grill. These 25 finalists came from all over the United States, including one from Hawaii. (He received a reverse reward—a trip to the mainland!) Two 1960 finalists had also won the trip in 1959.

The meat, groceries, and greengroceries had to be ordered ahead. Twenty-one different kinds of liquor were needed (for cooking purposes!), and 38 kinds of herbs and spices. Soy sauce, pineapple, garlic, ginger, sour cream, onions, lemons, and rice were in much demand, and of course butter, cream, and eggs—so necessary for good cooking—and the necessary fruits, vegetables, and sundries that were included in the yards and yards of grocery lists. Fortunately Hawaiian supermarkets are very super indeed. The fish, of course, was local and superb; so was the poultry and the pork. Beef comes from the mainland, frozen or "chilled." To be absolutely sure that each man got the cut he wanted, contestants were taken to market a full 24 hours before the Cookout. Items like sweet red onions, shallots, and Italian sausage were "imported" from California. One contestant who wanted unavailable Brazil nuts substituted Hawaiian macadamia nuts. He won the 1959 grand prize of $10,000!

Checking supplies, watching a demonstration of the grills, learning the rules, and advance recipe preparation were all done before the Big Day.

The cook-off! After breakfast the 25 contestants assembled in the cook-off area in the Ale Ale Kai Gardens. Each man was assigned a grill, a work table covered with quilted heavy-duty foil (for quick clean-up!), his gear, and his own shopping bag filled with the foods he had ordered. (Two more complete orders for each man were kept in nearby refrigerators, closely guarded.) They had from 10:30 to 3:30 in which to produce their masterpieces—one for photography, one for the judges, and a third only

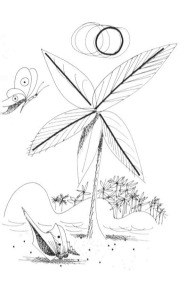

if they felt one of the first two could be improved upon. (They were a confident bunch—only one man cooked a third time.)

The judges were in a distant building, and as the food was finished to the satisfaction of each charcoal chef it was rushed to them for tasting. It took 90 seconds to be sped from grills to judges. In the cooking area only the contestants, a few officials, and some beautiful Polynesian girls—one for each five contestants—who stood ready to help in an emergency, were allowed. All during the cook-off there was music, talk of the contestants, their recipes, their backgrounds to keep the two to three thousand people who were watching from nearby bleachers informed of what was going on.

The cook-off was indeed a spectacular. When the white-clad contestants marched single file through the beautiful grounds to their grills, an awed and very temporary silence came over the onlookers. It was a beautiful sight—the lush green lawns, the magnificent palms and gorgeous tropical plants, the colorful flowers, the shipshape grills and shining work tables, made the whole scene unreal. But that was before the delectable odors started wafting from the grills!

The variety of the dishes cooked, as you will see from the recipes in this book, was great, and the judges knew that it was mighty good eating.

The judges were all celebrities. The first time, in 1959, they were Stan Musial, St. Louis Cardinal baseball star and owner of his own restaurant, Gaynor Maddox, Food & Markets Editor of NEA, Demetria Taylor, Food Editor of *Parade Magazine*, Dorothy Marsh, Director of Food and Cooking, *Good Housekeeping Magazine*, and Eleanor Crook, Food Editor, King Features Syndicate. Everyone was impressed with Stan Musial's charm, knowledge, and organizational ability. He was the natural leader. Gaynor Maddox is a colorful person; Demetria Taylor and Eleanor Crook knowing and pleasant, and Dorothy Marsh is a wonderfully warm personality, with great dignity. She delighted everyone by never appearing without a hat, even on a catamaran ride or at a cookout! The evening of the awards, another celebrity, James Garner of television fame, made the presentations. In 1960 the judges were Clementine Paddleford, popular Food Editor of *This Week*, Grace White, another dear person who is Food

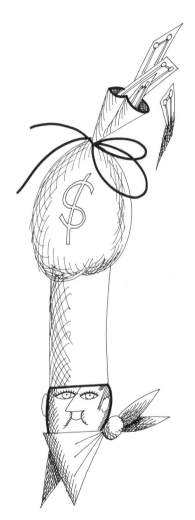

Editor of *Everywoman's Family Circle*, Mercedes Bates and Isabel Du-Bois, amiable and talented Food Editors of *McCall's* and *Chicago Daily News*, respectively, and Glenna McGinnis, of *Woman's Day*. Each went about her business conscientiously and efficiently, and came up with a winner. He, the winner, was awarded the check for $10,000 by motion picture star Joan Crawford Steele.

The American Cookout Champions of 1959 and 1960 had a great deal in common. They are both bachelors, both live alone in Southern California in homes with beautiful views, both are artists, and of course, both are superlative cooks! What's more, they are both named Robert.

Robert C. Gribbroeck, of 727 Linton Drive, Glendale, California, the 1959 winner, designs and paints backgrounds for Warner Brothers Cartoons. He was born in Rochester, New York, and attended the Academy of Fine Arts in Philadelphia, and the Rochester Institute of Technology in Rochester, New York. Mr. Gribbroek is a member of the Academy of Motion Picture Arts & Sciences. Besides barbecuing he likes weaving, gardening, and ceramics, and all of these hobbies contribute to the charm of his new-old home in Glendale, which he bought because the $10,000 grand prize enabled him to make the down payment.

Robert L. Balzer shows considerable talent in everything he undertakes. His hobbies—painting, photography, and writing—have often been an important part of his vocation. Born in Des Moines, Iowa, he came to Los Angeles as a small boy. His father was the owner of one of the country's great wine and food stores. After Bob graduated from Stanford and traveled and studied in Europe, he returned to help in the family business. Because of his knowledge of wine and food, he wrote his first book, *California's Best Wines*, in 1948. He used his skill with the camera to take photographs when serving as a special correspondent for United Press while traveling in Cambodia. The King of that country decorated him for his efforts in furthering better understanding between the United States and Cambodia. Mr. Balzer, who is now writing about travel and religion, used his grand prize money for his meditation center in Idyllwild, California.

The other winners, the four next highest contestants of each year, are

14

interesting men, too. They all won Jeep station wagons in addition to their gala trip for two. In 1959 they were:

Merritt H. Hursh of Pitman, New Jersey. He is an executive of the Maxwell Advertising Agency, and loves to hunt and cook.

Samuel G. Swisher was born in the beautiful Basque country of Oregon. He has traveled widely, is an ace salesman for Johnson & Johnson, and now lives in Phoenix, Arizona. He enjoys swimming, gardening, and hunting, and, of course, cooking.

Richard A. Wegener is a golfer and owner of a public relations firm in Fresno, California. He, too, likes to hunt and fish.

Richard B. Worl lives on beautiful Mercer Island in Washington, and is a district sales manager for Western Gear Corp. He enjoys yachting and swimming, as well as the popular hunting and golfing.

In 1960 the runners-up were:

Jerome M. Weakland of Walnut Creek, California, a sales engineer who also loves to cook, likes gardening and physical culture, too.

Jack Langston, of San Fernando, California, was born in Nevada. He has had many jobs in the movies, but is presently with Marquardt Corporation. He likes bowling and singing, as well as outdoor cooking.

John J. Barron, of North Abington, Massachusetts, is secretary and treasurer of a retail credit union. He has seven children and is an enthusiastic bowler and all-round outdoor sportsman.

Terry J. Strong, of Colorado Springs, Colorado, is an architectural draftsman. He enjoys stamp collecting and water-color painting.

What of these winning recipes? They, like the winners themselves, had a great deal in common, though they varied from rather elaborate flaming breasts of chicken to a simple beef roast cooked directly on the coals ("Roast on the Rocks," this was called). The common denominator was the imagination that was shown in the seasoning and the presentation, and the variety of flavors that were skillfully blended to a harmonious whole. Men, who frankly admit they are far better cooks than women, are inclined to use too many ingredients, feeling that if one herb makes it good, six should make it better. This fault was not apparent in these contributions. Though some were long—one having 24 ingredients—the component parts were always harmonious, never unnecessary. Some of the winning recipes were very elegant, some as simple as a new way to do hamburgers or hot dogs—all had distinction. In this book the 25 top ones from both cook-offs are included, as well as a number of others that certainly deserve honorable mention. We feel that they will all be of great value to anyone who enjoys cooking in the open.

Because the men who submitted these recipes were all experts, and do not go into the whys and wherefores of charcoal cookery, we here append some remarks upon the techniques of barbecue cooking.

How to Cook over Charcoal

THE COOK

IT IS OUR BELIEF that the cook should be male. Cooking over charcoal is a man's job and should have no interference from the distaff side of the family. If the man of the house *prefers* to have his wife do the cooking, just skip the whole idea of doing it outdoors. Nothing makes a man look —and we should think, feel—more henpecked than to have his wife officiate at the cookout. And if she happens to be wearing pants at the time, one reaches the obvious conclusion. So, men, do your own charcoal grilling and don't let your wife, mother-in-law, or even your best male friend tell you *how*. You are the boss and if you get too much unasked-for advice, simply walk away and leave the cooking to the mercy of the fire. Too many cooks spoil the cookout, too. Oh, let the women help, if you want to. Like peeling the onions and plucking the game birds and washing up after you. Of course, this only works if you have a slave for a wife, and there aren't as many of that type around as there used to be. The smart spouse will happily hand over the entire job to you, cleaning up and all, and if you are good at it, you'll prefer it that way. It will help to use quilted heavy-duty foil to cover your work table, as did the cook-off contestants; then just bunch it up and discard it when you've finished. Kaiser Broiler Pans are perfect for marinating meats and fish, and Kaiser 5-inch dishes, 8-inch layer cake pans, and loaf pans are deep enough to use for all types of mixing, and for cooking and serving vegetables, casseroles, and sauces. Use the 9-inch plates for serving. The broiler pans could also be used as plates, as could the trays if the meals are for young children or light eaters. All this will save much of the work of cleaning up after the cookout. Quilted heavy-duty foil is also invaluable for lining the fire boxes of all types of grills. You will notice that many of the contestants did just this, though it was not a requirement in the contests. That's because they know it will keep their fire boxes in tip-top shape and will give more heat, from reflection, from less fuel. And so the expert barbecue chefs will do the work themselves, without help from wife or friend, but with plenty from Kaiser Aluminum Foils.

EQUIPMENT

THE GRILL: Don't go all out buying an expensive charcoal grill unless you are sure that you and your family really enjoy cookouts. You can improvise one to begin with. Put a shelf from an old oven between 2 piles of bricks and build a fire underneath. You can broil on this as well as on the most expensive grill if you prop the shelf so that it is a wee bit higher in front than in back, and the grids run from front to back (more of this later). Or you can use a *wok* (an iron Chinese frying pan) or any large shallow metal pan. Place a grill on top of it. It is wise to line these with quilted heavy-duty foil and put sand or volcanic ash in the bottom to keep the heat from burning out the pan, and making the use of a shallower fire possible. Of course, these grills are for broiling only. If you want to roast over charcoal, you will need a spit, preferably one driven by an electric motor. Inexpensive ones are to be had. If you decide you want a better grill, they are readily available, variously priced from about 15 to 200 dollars. The best ones have an adjustable firebox or grate (or both), a hood to keep heat in and cold breezes out, and are engineered so that the grids slant towards troughs which catch the grease, preventing flare-ups.

THE WORK TABLE: You really need a good-sized work table, though some grills have large enough shelves so that you can dispense with a table if absolutely necessary. As we have said, covering the table with quilted heavy-duty foil will help when it's time to clean up.

OTHER GEAR: Indispensable gear includes *asbestos mitts* or gloves, for adjusting the balance of the meat when the spit is hot, and for handling hot pans and even coals; *tongs* for turning food when broiling (see below) and for adding charcoal when needed; *sprinkling bottle* for dousing the fire, though if you are a good barbecue cook this is seldom necessary; *pliers* for tightening holding forks on the spit. *Hinged broilers:* these are invalu-

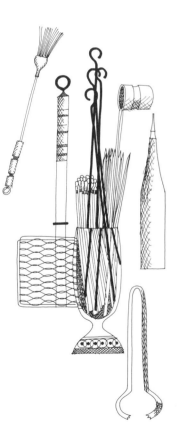

able for broiling small pieces of meat or fish, such as shrimps, trout and kidneys. It is nice to have one with small grids, one with larger ones. *Basket broilers* are also useful. They have sides so that food cannot slip out of the broiler. They are good for plump hamburgers, sweetbreads, and other foods that you don't want compressed, and for lobsters, whole fish, and such. Hinged broilers of any kind make fast work of turning, too. *Basting brushes:* You can use a bunch of parsley or other herbs for this purpose, but a long-handled brush is easier and neater. The basting sauce can be kept in a jar or in a Kaiser Aluminum Loaf Pan. *Drip pans:* these are essential for all spit-roasting. Placed in the front of the fire, they will catch all the drippings so that there will be no flare-up. Pans to fit your spit are easily made by folding doubled quilted heavy-duty foil into the proper long narrow size, and turning up the edges to make a pan about 1½ inches deep. *Thermometers:* a meat thermometer may seem sissy to some men cooks, but actually it is invaluable if you like rare roast beef (see below). *Skewers:* If you plan to cook shish kabob or anything *en brochette,* you will need these. Long metal ones with or without wooden handles are good for large pieces of meat, but small bamboo skewers can be used for small tidbits, such as chicken livers or oysters or meat balls. The wooden ones should first be soaked in water so they won't burn. *Knives:* Every good meat cook deserves a really fine carving knife. Of course, he can take it from the house supply. It should be kept razor-sharp, and the best way to do this is to have it ground professionally once a year, and to sharpen it on a steel frequently. Other knives for boning, meat cutting, and vegetable preparation are also useful, but they, too, can be borrowed from the kitchen. *Carving board:* A good one is a must; knives last much longer if meat is carved on a board. A *cutting board* for pre-cooking use is also a necessity.

Extra gear: Nice but not necessary are such things as long-handled forks and spoons for outdoor cooking, special large salt and pepper mills, fancy aprons, condiment trays, and special pot holders. A large towel has pinch-hit for many an apron, and they are also useful for holding pots and for hurried mopping-up.

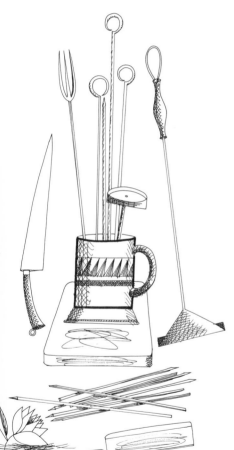

FUEL

Almost without question the fuel will be charcoal, though any sweet-smelling wood such as fruit or nut is wonderful. Charcoal should be made from hardwood, and usually is. Most outdoor cooks prefer charcoal briquets, with good reason; because they are of uniform size they burn more evenly. However, there is a great difference in them, as some are made of hardwood, some of anthracite, some of fruit pits, and some of heaven knows what. (It is not our place to recommend a brand, though we have our favorite. Suffice it to say that it is made of hardwood.) Some briquets have so much filler that they retain their shape even after they are burned out. Some burn very hot, some just the opposite, so don't try a new fuel if you are having a party and the timing must be exact.

FIRE-MAKING

Many thousands of words have been written and millions more spoken on this subject. It used to be a very controversial one, but today there are such quick and efficient ways of doing the job that the advocate of the old camper's method of building a tepee with kindling wood and adding heavier wood as it burns is apt to get laughed off the cookout area. Now, if an electric outlet is nearby, an electric fire starter is often used. It is quick and efficient. Another very good way is to make use of a liquid fire lighter—either one made for the purpose or an odorless paint thinner, which is much less expensive. Pile a few briquets in a high heap, douse with the liquid, and light. Even better, have a covered can in which a few briquets are kept soaking in paint thinner. Use a few of these in the bottom of your pile of briquets or fire chimney. (A fire chimney is a wonderful gadget that can be made from a 46-ounce tomato juice can or a 2-pound coffee can. With a beer can opener make 4 holes in the sides near the bottom of the can. Remove top and bottom and put "chimney" on the fire bed. In the chimney put several marinated briquets, then add plain briquets to the top, or as many as you'll need for the culinary project at hand. Light and let burn until all the briquets are glowing well.

Remove chimney, using tongs or asbestos gloves.) Spread the fire in the manner desired, adding more briquets around the edges if the cooking period is to be a long one; as they ignite they can be raked into position.

SIZE OF FIRE

Many novices and even some old hands make much larger fires than necessary. This is wasteful, because charcoal is an expensive fuel. For a small hibachi-type grill, not more than 6 or 8 briquets will be needed; for a larger grill from 3 to 5 times that amount. (For instance, 36 to 40 briquets will suffice to broil steaks on a standard 18-by-20-inch grill.) For large roasts, add briquets around the edge, as above. The fire is ready to use when the briquets are all burning and a little white ash is beginning to show.

SHAPE OF FIRE

For broiling, the fire should be about the size and shape of the grill that is used, unless you are using only a small portion of the grill, in which case have it the size of that space. If the food is small or thin and will cook quickly, the briquets may be spaced quite far apart. If, however, the food is thick, have a solid bed of coals.

FLARING

If flaring does occur, either from fat from the meat or from an oily baste dripping into the fire, douse it with water from a sprinkling bottle or a spray gun, or even a whisk broom dipped in water. However, as we keep saying, a good outdoor cook with a well-engineered grill, won't have much flaring. Some cooks advocate a circle of coals, around the edge of the food to be cooked. This does eliminate flare-up, as it's the dripping fat hitting the coals that makes the flames, but we don't think it cooks as evenly. Besides, we have a better method of flare control.

IN SPIT-ROASTING the fire should be as long as the spit, and should be

built toward the rear of the firebox with the drip pan in front. If the spit turns properly—away from you at the top, towards you at the bottom—the fat will drip off into the pan at the front of the firebox. (If you are to the right of the fire, facing the end of the spit, it should be turning clockwise.) The reason for this is that the fat does not drip directly at the bottom of the turn, but a little afterwards, thus falling into the pan rather than the fire. Thus you'll have no flaring and can let a roast cook for an hour or more unattended.

HEAT CONTROL

This is easy if you know how and there's no reason why you shouldn't. It's just a matter of learning how hot your fuel burns, how large a fire to build, and how to maintain an even temperature. When your fire is ready, gauge its heat by holding your hand over it at cooking level and counting off seconds—you know, Mississippi one, Mississippi two, Mississippi three, and so on. With a slow fire you will be able to hold your hand in place for 4 seconds, with a very hot fire only 1 second. You can figure out the in-betweens. If the fire is too hot, you simply raise the grill farther from the fire, if not hot enough, lower it closer to the source of the heat. Some barbecues have stationary grills and fireboxes that are adjustable, but the control is the distance between fire and grill. If you are way off in your judgment of fire size, you'll just have to add briquets and wait until they are burning, or if the fire is too hot, spread the coals or even douse some with water. If your food needs a tiny bit more cooking and the fire is burning low, you can generate extra heat by brushing the ashes from the top of the coals.

TEMPERATURES

There are four temperatures that have to be taken into consideration in cooking out-of-doors. Because three of them make a great deal of difference in the length of time needed for cooking, and the fourth tells when the food is done to your taste, they are of utmost importance.

TEMPERATURE OF THE AIR: If it is cold, it will naturally take longer to cook. This can be partially controlled by the use of a grill with a hood, especially if there is a cold wind blowing.

TEMPERATURE OF THE FOOD: With large pieces of meat for roasting, such as rib roast or turkey or suckling pig, it is very important to have the meat at room temperature before starting to cook. This is also true of thick steaks and chops, especially if you want them rare. To cook thinner steaks rare, it is better to have them very cold if you want a char on the outside. The only possible way to cook a really thin steak—say ½-inch thick— rare and still have a nice brown outside, is to have the meat frozen and the fire very hot. We don't recommend frozen meat as a rule, but we know that many people depend on it, so all we can advise is that you cook it in its frozen state unless you want all the juices to thaw away. With poultry it's different; thaw and bring to room temperature, as above. In any case, make allowances for the temperature of the meat when figuring on time. All the times given in this Introduction apply to meat at room temperature, or about 70 degrees throughout.

TEMPERATURE OF THE FIRE: This is pretty well covered under Fire-Making and Heat Control. We might add here that you should have a medium fire for cooking large pieces of meat (temperature at the spit level not over 300°); a hot fire for steaks if you like a well-browned outside and the steaks are under 2 inches thick; a slow to medium fire for roast pork, spareribs, and the like.

TEMPERATURE OF THE COOKED MEAT: This is where your meat thermometer comes in. And we will risk the wrath of most recipe writers in this country by saying they are all wrong in their recommended temperatures. For instance, they say 140° internal temperature is *rare*. We don't even think it's medium rare—medium, yes. And what do we call rare? Not more than 130°, while we think very rare is closer to 120°. In the second place, meat goes on cooking after it is removed from the heat, the thermometer sometimes climbing as much as 10 degrees. So cook that beautiful standing rib roast at 140° and chances are you'll not even have it medium, but well done. But you'll have to decide for yourselves. Get a *good* meat thermometer—one that registers from 0° to 200° F. is best—and use it to test the internal temperature of the meat both before and after cooking.

MARINATING AND BASTING

Some meats, especially tough cuts, need marinating. Others are better, we think, without such treatment. Marinating, particularly in wine or vinegar, does have a tenderizing effect. It also adds flavor, and when meat is marinated too long it overpowers the flavor of the meat. This, apparently, is a joy to those who have venison but do not like its gamey taste, but most of us prefer our meat to taste like what it is. The same is true of basting, though not as definitely. Too highly flavored a basting sauce will, however, kill the delicacy of many foods, so take it easy.

Basic Recipes for Outdoor Cooking

CHARCOAL BROILING

Steaks: Steak is still the favorite meat for a cookout, even though anything that can be broiled or roasted indoors can, and is, cooked at the charcoal grill. Selecting the steak takes thought as well as money. There are several choices. Individual steaks, such as T-bone, porterhouse, club, strip, or, if you like them, tenderloin steaks, are popular with many, but we feel they have one drawback. To be good they should be thick, and a whole one is too much for light eaters, and perhaps not enough for trenchermen. A wonderful solution is to buy a large thick sirloin steak and slice it after it is cooked. Thus each maid and man can have the just-right-size serving. We'd allow ¾ pound per person of this cut.

To cook: Have a good hot fire for steaks if you want a char—and most people do want some crispness on the outside of their steaks. What's more, everybody must prefer the fat to be brown and crinkly. (If not, he might as well bake the steaks in a slow oven!) If the grids on your grill don't slant, prop up the front an inch or so; the melting fat will run down the grids to the back and you can make a long narrow trough of quilted heavy-duty foil to place in the rear of the fire to catch these drippings. Result: no flare-up. But wait! If you want a really black char, and some profess to do so, let the fire flame around the meat. There is another problem: those who want a brown but not black exterior and a well-done interior. The solution is to achieve the desired color, then slip a sheet of quilted heavy-duty foil under the steak and continue cooking until it is done to your liking. As for seasoning, brush with a basting sauce, if you wish, though we advocate plain salt and pepper, sprinkled on after the steak is cooked. Some cooks howl with rage if anyone turns a steak with a fork, insisting that the juices are lost. They use tongs. We disagree. Never yet have we seen any sign of juice run from a partially cooked steak, and we have deliberately pierced one in several places to prove our point. But no matter

—use what comes naturally for turning the meat. Now as to timing. That is tough, as we have already stated. However, taking all the above-mentioned temperatures into consideration, we give you the following as a partial guide: a 1-inch steak should cook *very rare* in 3 to 4 minutes on a side; a 1½-inch one in 4 to 6 minutes on a side; a 2-inch one in 8 to 10 minutes on a side; and a 2½-inch steak in from 10 to 15 minutes on a side. Treat a thicker one like a roast. For *rare*, a 1-inch steak should cook 4 to 5 minutes on a side; a 1½-inch one 5 to 7 minutes; a 2-inch one 9 to 15 minutes on a side; and a 2½-inch one 12 to 18 minutes on a side. For *medium* steaks, a 1-inch one should cook for 5 to 8 minutes on a side; a 1½-inch one 7 to 9 minutes on a side; a 2-inch one 12 to 18 minutes; and a 2½-inch steak should cook for 18 to 23 minutes on a side. To cook steaks *well done* is harder to define. We suppose that people who want their meat that way object to the slightest tinge of pink. So for a 1-inch steak try 9 or 10 minutes on a side; a 1½-inch one 10 to 15 minutes; a 2-inch one 18 to 25 minutes; and a 2½-inch one 35 minutes on a side. (These long cooking times break our hearts, but we will suffer just for you few.) As you see, there is plenty of leeway in these times, so we suggest that when the shortest time is reached, you make a slit near the bone (if there is one!) using a very sharp knife. Take a look, and if the meat isn't done enough, return it to the grill.

London broil: This steak, featured at fine restaurants, is good only when cooked very rare. The humble flank steak, usually rolled and braised for a long time because of its so-called toughness, is used, and the reason it is tender is because it *is* rare. Try broiling it well done and you'll have a splendid candidate for a doormat. Cook and carve it according to these directions and you'll have one of the most deliciously tender, juicy, flavorsome steaks that you have ever tasted. Select a Prime or Choice Grade flank steak, and have it skinned but *not* scored. Brush with oil or melted butter or, if you prefer, with Baste No. 1, and cook for 3 to 5 minutes on each side, depending upon the size of the steak. (You'll need a good hot fire for this.) Put on a board, carve in very thin crosswise diagonal slices. If you slant the knife properly and make really diagonal slices, each one will be about

$2\frac{1}{2}$ to 3 inches wide—a beautiful juicy red with a slight edging of brown.

STEAKS OTHER THAN BEEF: Lamb steaks, cut from the leg, and venison steaks are also good broiled. Do them in exactly the same way as the beef steaks. As for degree of doneness, we are opinionated about that, too. We believe that lamb steaks should be rare (not *very* rare) or possibly medium rare (between rare and medium, if you use our time recommendations for steaks). They are far better that way than well done, as they are so often served. We feel the same way about venison. (If your venison is from a tough old buck, don't broil it but braise it; here is a case where marinating often helps to tenderize the meat.) If you disagree with us, you probably do so violently and will suit yourself anyway.

HAM STEAKS: Center cuts of ham are delicious when cooked over charcoal, but they must not be too thin. Anything less than $\frac{3}{4}$ inch will dry out. Gash the fat around the edge of the ham, brush with melted butter or Bastes No. 3 or 4 (see following), and broil over a low fire, basting occasionally. The ham should be nicely browned and, of course, thoroughly cooked. The modern tenderized or precooked hams are best for broiling as the cooking time is short.

CHOPS: We don't believe that a chop less than $\frac{3}{4}$ inch thick is worth broiling, and we prefer them thicker. We also think lamb chops, like lamb steaks, should be cooked rare, though pork chops must have longer cooking. However, pork should be juicy even though well done, so watch them carefully while broiling. For a $\frac{3}{4}$-inch-thick chop allow 2 minutes on a side for rare, 3 or 4 minutes on a side for medium rare, 5 to 8 minutes on a side for medium, and 8 to 11 minutes on a side for well done. For 1-inch chops allow 3 minutes on a side for rare, 4 to 7 minutes on a side for medium rare, 8 to 10 minutes on a side for medium, and 10 to 13 minutes on a side for well done. For a $1\frac{1}{2}$-inch chop allow 4 to 5 minutes on a side for rare, 5 to 8 minutes on a side for medium rare, 9 to 12 minutes on a side for medium, and 12 to 15 minutes on a side for well done.

ROAST SPARERIBS: We believe that the very best way to cook spareribs is to roast them on a spit. In order to do this they must be purchased in one piece (or two or three, depending upon how many you wish to serve; we allow 1 pound of spareribs for each person.) Marinate in Bastes No. 3 or 4 for several hours, or use this Chinesey one: Combine ½ cup each of soy sauce, orange juice, and sherry; add 3 tablespoons of grated fresh (or crystallized) ginger, 2 puréed cloves of garlic, and ¼ cup each of honey and oil. (Spareribs are also wonderful plain, with salt and pepper only.) Weave the marinated ribs on the spit and cook from 1 to 1½ hours, or until shiny, the fat crisply brown, and the meat fork-tender. You may baste with the marinade mixture while the spareribs are cooking, but it isn't really necessary. As the fat doesn't fall into the fire (if you've listened to us, that is!) you don't have to watch the ribs while they are cooking.

BROILED SPARERIBS: If you haven't a spit, or prefer to do the spareribs right on the grill, cut them into 1- or 2- or 3-rib pieces and marinate as above. Broil over a fairly low fire, turning frequently, until done. This should take about an hour. You may baste during the cooking, but if you do, watch for flaring and douse the fire quickly if it occurs. You don't want black ribs. Sometimes the ribs are perfectly colored before they are tender. If this happens, wrap them in quilted heavy-duty foil and continue cooking until done. You can fork-test them right through the foil.

HAMBURGERS: Hamburgers are wonderful when broiled over charcoal. Just make them as usual, but perhaps a bit larger and thicker (we make 3 hamburgers from each pound of ground beef) and broil them until they're done to your liking. (We won't give you timing here—it's easy enough to peek!) Of course, you can add monosodium glutamate, chopped onion, puréed garlic, pepper and salt, red wine (¼ cup to each pound of meat), or whatever you like before cooking, but we like them best handled lightly, cooked rare (as if you hadn't guessed!) and seasoned after cooking.

HAMBURG VARIATIONS: Besides the seasonings we suggest above, we think you might enjoy the sandwich type of hamburger. Make 2 thin cakes instead of 1 thick one, and put them together with a slice of onion, a piece of cheese, or perhaps some pickle relish. Press the edges down firmly and broil. Another trick we like is to put a slice of butter and a few chips of ice between the two layers—this makes for extra juiciness.

HAMBURG STEAKS: You can form ground beef into a large steak-sized oval and broil it whole, then cut in portions for serving. This can be quite elegant, if you serve a Béarnaise or mushroom sauce with it. It is also good when topped with fried onions or with melted butter to which a few capers have been added.

BROILED KIDNEYS: Spilt lamb kidneys almost in half, remove cores, and open flat. Thread skewers through them so that they will remain flat, brush with melted butter or oil, and broil from 6 to 14 minutes. If you overcook them, they will toughen. Sprinkle with salt and pepper, pour on a little melted butter, and enjoy.

KABOB COOKERY: This, of course, is meat or other things strung on skewers and broiled. The most famous is the *shish kabob* of the Near East. That is usually lamb or mutton, cut in good-sized chunks, marinated in olive oil, salt and pepper, then strung on skewers, alternating with tomatoes cut in wedges, onions cut the same way, and squares of green pepper. (Cut this way they stay on the skewers better, but in Near and Middle Eastern countries the vegetables are often sliced.) This method of cookery has been borrowed freely, and today almost anything is strung on skewers and called a kabob. Sometimes the marinade is more elaborate, like Marinade No. 1, and often mushrooms or pieces of eggplant are strung on the skewers along with the meat. The latter can be anything: beef, turkey chunks, venison, fish, shrimps, pork, kidneys, liver, oysters . . . we could go on and on. These may or may not be combined with vegetables or even fruit. Other kabobs are strictly vegetarian, being skewers filled with vegetables or fruit. These often make a good accompaniment to meats broiled or roasted in another manner. The filled skewers are cooked over a medium fire and should be turned frequently. Do not overcook. If the meat is juicily pink we think you'll like it better—at least, we hope so.

TERIYAKI: This is another way of using skewers, usually ones made of bamboo. (They are pre-soaked in water to keep them from burning.) Use Baste No. 4 (see following) for a marinade, adding sugar if you like that authentic Japanese flavor with your meat. Thin slices of steak, either cut in squares and strung on the skewers, or in long strips and woven on them, are a favorite, especially as an appetizer. But like kabobs, there are many variations of this cooking method. Pork is often used, and so are chicken livers, shrimps, and anything else that seems like a good idea. Pineapple chunks and kumquats appear strung between the meat, and even stuffed green olives, though they are certainly not Oriental. In other words, you're on your own! Teriyaki, because the pieces of meat are small, is perfect for hibachi cookery. You'll need very few briquets and the cooking time is remarkably quick.

CHARCOAL ROASTING

We have already described how to make and control the fire for spit-roasting. The other important phase of charcoal roasting is the proper balance of the meat on the spit. If it is out of balance, the spit will turn jerkily or may even stop. If the meat is compactly and evenly shaped, as in a rolled rib roast or a whole tenderloin, this is very simple. Other pieces should be spitted, as nearly as possible, through their centers of gravity. For example, a standing rib roast should have the spit go through the meat at a slant, inserting towards the small end (near the bone ends) and having it emerge towards the top of the large end (thus angling in two directions, from side to side and from bottom to top). A whole turkey should be securely trussed, then spitted through the back in front of the tail (just above the spot where the oil sack was), with the spit emerging through the end of the breast bone (usually just below the top of the wishbone, although the center of gravity in turkeys varies somewhat). To make sure that the meat is properly balanced, put one end of the spit on the palm of each hand, or on two props of equal size. If it doesn't turn, it is probably balanced, but just to make sure, give the meat a quarter turn, then a half turn. When it still balances, you're in, and the spit can be inserted in its socket and the motor started. (If this balancing is done well ahead of time, it will save a lot of last-minute confusion.) It would be nice if we could say that your balancing troubles are now over, but such is not the case. As the fat renders out and the meat "firms," it may have to be rebalanced. Fortunately, many grills now have compensating weights that can be added (or removed). (This is the same principle as balancing a wheel on your car.) But let's get on to the roasting.

RIB ROAST OF BEEF: A standing roast of at least 3 ribs is one of the most majestic and impressive of sights as it turns to a crispy brown perfection over a charcoal fire. Do not try to gauge its degree of doneness by its weight. As the diameter of a 3-rib roast is much the same as one of 7 ribs, there is little difference in the cooking time, though naturally the first ribs, or small end, take a little less. If you want your roast very rare, at an internal temperature of 120 to 130 degrees, cook from 1¾ to 2¼ hours; if you want the meat rare—130 to 140 degrees, cook from 2 to 2½ hours; medium—140 to 150—from 2¼ to 3 hours; and well done—150 to 170 degrees—from 3 to 4 hours. (This is for a 4-rib roast). If you use a thermometer, remember to stop cooking when it has reached 5 degrees *under* your preferred temperature. It will cook that much more after the heat is removed. It is a good idea to douse the fire or crank it way down and cover it with a double layer of quilted heavy-duty foil, and let the meat continue to turn on the spit to develop the juices and finish the cooking. We usually salt the meat towards the end of the cooking, but never, never baste it.

ROLLED RIB ROAST: Cook this just as you do the standing rib roast. It may take slightly longer to cook, as the bones induct the heat and thus carry it to the center.

SPENCER ROAST: Some say this is a rib roast with the bones removed. Others say it is the "eye" of the roast, that lean tender circle of meat that runs through the center of the roast. In either case, cook just as you would the other roasts. We have cooked a 16-pound one in 1½ hours. It was, of course, blood rare.

WHOLE TENDERLOIN OF BEEF: This can be roasted on the spit or, if you're not blessed with one, cooked like a steak, on the grill. Roasted it will take 25 to 30 minutes for very rare, and to cook it well done is, we feel, gastronomical heresy. If broiled, treat it like a steak of equal thickness.

ROAST LEG OF LAMB: This is another favorite for roasting over charcoal. Run the spit parallel to the bone, and balance. If you wish, you may tuck a few slivers of garlic into slits that you've made in the meat. Baste with a mixture of equal parts of red wine and oil, well flavored with rosemary. Or use Baste No. 1 or 3. An average-sized leg of lamb will take from 1 to 1½ hours to cook rare, 1½ hours medium rare, and up to 2½ hours to reach the well-done stage.

BONED LEG OF LAMB: This may be tied in a compact form and roasted on the spit, as above, or it may be opened out flat and broiled like a steak, for 45 minutes to 1 hour. Delicious!

BONED SHOULDER OF LAMB: Do just like the boned leg of lamb, but on a spit. It does not adapt well to broiling because it has to be tied to hold in shape.

ROAST LOIN OF PORK: This is pork at its best, if it's roasted over a slow fire and cooked to juicy perfection. It will take from 2 to 2½ hours to cook to 175°. The meat may be sprinkled with salt, pepper, and oregano half way through the cooking, to give extra flavor to the wonderfully crispy outside.

ROAST TURKEY: Stuff or not, as you wish. Also baste if you wish (No. 2 is a good one), but it is not necessary. Be careful in balancing (see above) and readjust balance when necessary. A 16-pound turkey will take about 3 hours to cook, slightly longer if stuffed. It is done if, when pricked with a fork, the juices run clear, and when the leg moves easily at the joint.

ROAST DUCK: A domestic duck will roast in 1 to 1½ hours. A wild duck, if you like it blood rare, in 15 minutes—allow more time if you want them better done. In either case, stuffing is unnecessary, but it is a nice idea to put a slice of onion, a rib of celery, and perhaps a piece of apple in the cavity before cooking.

ROAST GOOSE: Because it is very fat, a goose should be pricked a few times during the cooking. It will take from 1¾ to 3 hours, depending on its size.

ROAST CHICKEN: Don't try to spit-roast a chicken under 4 pounds. The

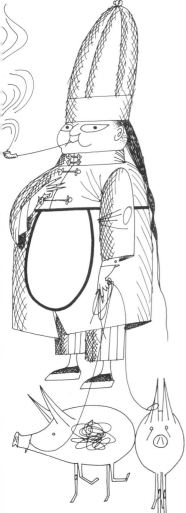

smaller ones are better broiled. For roasting, stuff or not, as desired, and cook from 1 to 1½ hours, basting, if you wish, as for turkey.

ROAST LIVER: If you like veal or baby beef liver, you will find this a great treat. Have a 4- or 5-pound piece of liver tied in a compact form, and larded. Spit and cook until you have an internal temperature of 150°, which will be pinkly juicy. Slice and serve.

ROAST BABY PIG: Here's a gala dish if ever there was one! Select a pig weighing from 12 to 30 pounds and make sure that it is not too long for your spit. (We once made that mistake and had to cut the little dear in two, and cook him on two grills!) Leave the head on; rub cavity with salt, and return the liver, kidneys, and heart to the inside. Sew up and tie legs together. Spit from right shoulder to left ham, on a long diagonal. Rub all over with butter and start cooking, basting with more melted butter, or with Baste No. 2 or 4 (see following). A whole pig will cook faster than you think. A small one will usually be done in 2 hours, and we have cooked a 29-pound one to perfection in 3½ hours.

GAME: Game may be broiled or roasted just like beef. As we have explained before, it often needs marinating. Marinade No. 1 (see following) is a good one. If you like rare beef and the flavor of venison, you'll like it cooked rare. If you don't, we're sorry it's wasted on you!

FISH: Although a large whole fish can be spit-roasted, it's rather tricky. It has to be wrapped in wire netting or tied in many places to keep it from falling off the spit. We prefer to split and broil it, or to have it sliced in steaks and broil those. Small fish can be broiled whole. In all cases, do take care not to overcook it. We don't attempt to give times as many different conditions are involved. You can tell when a fish is done very easily; it loses that translucent look, and the flakes separate easily when poked with a fork. Basting of fish is usually a good idea. We like Baste No. 2, 3, and 4 (see following) for this purpose.

BROILED SHRIMP: Jumbo shrimps, or prawns as they are called in some parts of the country, are delectable when broiled. Leave the shells on but, using a pointed pair of scissors, split down the back and rinse out the black vein. Marinate in Baste No. 4 (or 3 or 2) then, using a hinged broiler with small grids, or threading the shrimps on skewers, broil from 2 to 3 minutes on each side. Serve in the shells with plenty of paper napkins or, better, with towels wrung out in hot water in the Oriental manner.

BROILED LOBSTER: Although most cooks split live lobsters before broiling them, we find that results in some loss of those heavenly juices. So we broil them whole. A small lobster will take from 12 to 15 minutes to cook. Split at once, remove stomach, and serve with prodigal amounts of melted butter. If you prefer splitting the lobsters first, do so. Remove stomach and intestinal vein and cook, flesh side down, for 2 or 3 minutes. Turn, lave generously with butter, and cook another 8 to 12 minutes, depending upon size of the lobster. The flesh will be opaque when done. Serve with more butter and lemon.

Bastes and Marinades

A MARINADE is a thin seasoned sauce in which meats and sometimes seafoods are marinated or soaked before cooking. A baste is a seasoned sauce which is brushed or squirted on the food while it is cooking.

BASTE NO. 1: Combine 1 cup of red wine, 1 cup of oil, 1 teaspoon of salt, some freshly ground pepper, and 1 teaspoon of rosemary or marjoram. A puréed clove of garlic may also be used. Good for all red meat and game, and also good on chicken and game birds.

BASTE NO. 2: Make like Baste No. 1, but substitute white wine for the red, tarragon or thyme for the herbs. Good for chicken, turkey, and fish.

BASTE NO. 3: Combine 1 cup each of vermouth (French or Italian) and olive oil; add 2 tablespoons of lemon juice. This is good for almost anything but especially for lamb chops or roast.

BASTE NO. 4: Combine equal parts of soy sauce, sherry, and a bland oil, such as peanut. Add puréed garlic and/or grated ginger to taste. This has an Oriental quality, and is good on pork, chicken, shrimps, veal, beef.

BASTE NO. 5: Combine 1 cup of tomato catsup, 1 cup of red wine, 2 puréed cloves of garlic, 2 tablespoons each of vinegar and Worcestershire sauce, 1 teaspoon each of sugar and salt, and Tabasco to your taste. This is the kind of a hot baste that used to be very popular. It is usually called "barbecue sauce" and is used by its devotees on steaks, chops, roasts, chickens, hamburgers, and whatever they don't really *like* the taste of.

MARINADE NO. 1: Combine 2 cups of red wine, 1/2 cup of red wine vinegar, 1 cup of chopped onion, an herb bouquet consisting of bay, parsley, and thyme, and a few crushed peppercorns. Simmer 5 minutes, and cool befor using. For red meats and game.

MARINADE NO. 2: Make like Marinade No. 1, but use white wine instead of red, and white wine vinegar. Use for all poultry.

NOTE: Bastes No. 3 and 4 may also be used for marinades.

Barbecue Entertaining

EVEN THOUGH A COOKOUT PARTY is the easiest possible way to entertain, it still takes a little planning. Sometimes the men do it all, more often they leave everything but the actual charcoal cooking to the ladies, who will plan what other foods to serve. It's up to them to decide on appetizers, if any (chances are that the man will attend to the drinks, or delegate some friend to do so), and approximately what time the meal should be served. She'll have to find out from the cook how long his masterpiece will take, and have her dishes coördinated accordingly. We won't go into appetizers here, for this is not a general cookbook. Serve what is easiest and remember that the cocktail hour may last a long time if the cook has misjudged his timing, so allow plenty of possible leeway. But don't let everyone fill up on hors d'oeuvre, and you know why.

THE MENU: The dish cooked at the grill will be, of course, the *pièce de résistance*, but it will need accompaniments—a starchy casserole, perhaps, and roast corn and/or potatoes. A salad, too, is usually in order, and so is bread occasionally. Hot garlic bread is a great favorite, but because of that it gets a little tiresome. Beer or wine is very often served at a cookout, and of course coffee *always* finishes off the feast. As for dessert, almost anything goes. Below we give some suggestions of what to serve with various cookout dishes. We have kept the accompaniments simple so that you can find the recipes in any standard cookbook. If you want more elegant and exotic menus, you can have fun creating your own.

STEAK: Potatoes au gratin; sliced tomatoes sprinkled with oregano and served with an oil and vinegar dressing; homemade bread, toasted on a fork over the coals; strawberries and cream or strawberry shortcake.

LONDON BROIL: Fried onions; hashed brown potatoes with sesame seeds; green beans vinaigrette; fresh peach pie.

LAMB STEAKS OR CHOPS: Rice pilaf; broiled eggplant (or eggplant casserole); fresh fruit salad; crackers and cheese.

Ham steaks: Charcoal-broiled corn or corn pudding; foil-wrapped yams roasted in the ashes; pickled apricots; cole slaw; fresh pears with Roquefort cheese.

Spareribs: Fried rice; corn bread; orange salad; chocolate cake.

Hamburgers & hamburg steaks: Hamburgers just have to have buns, but make them extra good by toasting and buttering. Have sliced onion, sliced tomato, lettuce, sliced cheese, and relish to suit all tastes. For dessert how about chocolate nut sundaes and angel food cake? Serve hamburg steak as suggested in the recipe. With it have fried potatoes and cole slaw, with fresh fruit, crackers, and cheese for dessert; or kidney bean salad, onion rolls, and watermelon.

Broiled liver steaks: Fried onions and/or broiled mushrooms would be good here, also shoestring potatoes, avocado salad, and deep-dish apple pie with cheese.

Broiled chicken: Risotto; onions roasted in foil; mixed green salad; fresh blueberry cake.

Shish kabobs: Cracked wheat pilaf and cracker bread should be enough with the vegetables in the shish kabobs. For dessert have strawberries dressed with honey and sour cream, and small sweet cookies.

Rib roast of beef: Foil-roasted potatoes with chive-flavored butter; peas cooked in foil; horseradish and sour cream sauce; hard rolls; Caesar salad; fresh pineapple with rum.

Whole tenderloin of beef: Foil-cooked mushrooms in butter; rice with chopped pecans; raw spinach salad; raspberry sherbet with fresh raspberries and whipped cream.

Roast leg of lamb: New potatoes browned in butter; asparagus salad; Sacher torte.

Roast loin of pork: Spoon bread; apples roasted in foil; lima beans cooked in foil; cold strawberry soufflé.

Roast turkey: Onion tart; cranberry sauce; sweet potatoes roasted in foil; romaine and cress salad; fresh peach ice cream.

ROAST DUCK: Brown or wild rice with buttered crumbs; sliced onions roasted in foil; currant jelly; blueberry muffins; lemon meringue pie.

ROAST CHICKEN: Succotash cooked in foil; creamed potatoes in casserole; combination salad; chocolate roll.

ROAST LIVER: Onions roasted in foil; broiled tomatoes; shoestring potatoes; cheese cake.

ROAST BABY PIG: Hominy spoon bread; fried apple slices; green beans cooked in foil; celery salad; cantaloupe.

BROILED FISH: Foil-roasted potatoes with cheese sauce; toasted rye bread; cucumbers in sour cream with dill; fresh coconut layer cake or Napoleons.

BROILED SHRIMPS: Rice with peas; toasted French bread with sesame seed butter; mixed green salad; date torte with whipped cream, or cream puffs with caramel sauce.

BROILED LOBSTER: French fried potatoes reheated in foil; cole claw with green peppers; cherry tomatoes; hot cheese bread; pineapple shell with fresh fruits and kirsch or Cointreau.

That does it except to stress that the reason cookouts are such fun is that they are little work. In the menus above we suggest much foil cooking—that is to save pans. (Frozen vegetables with a bit of butter and salt and pepper, folded into a packet of quilted heavy-duty foil, will cook over the grill in a short time; fresh vegetables will take a little longer.) Use paper tablecloths and paper napkins—outdoors is one place where everybody expects them—and keep tableware at a minimum. Go to town on gay decorations—wild flowers, fruit, even colorful vegetables can decorate the tables. And don't hesitate to ask your guests to help with the few chores there are. That is part of the fun.

Happy Cookouts!

HELEN EVANS BROWN
PHILIP S. BROWN

Pasadena, 1961

40

The Cookout Book

Rib Eye on the Spit

5- to 6-pound eye of rib roast
½ cup salad oil
½ cup soy sauce
½ cup bourbon whiskey
2 small onions, thinly sliced
2 cloves garlic, chopped

2 tablespoons fresh ginger, chopped
(or 3 tablespoons preserved
ginger)
1 teaspoon freshly ground pepper
1 teaspoon dry mustard
¼ cup wine vinegar

Combine all marinade ingredients, pour over roast and let stand in this mixture for 1 hour, turning frequently. ❧ Prepare fire of charcoal briquets at least 30 minutes before you are ready to barbecue. Soak 2 large handfuls of hickory chips in water for 30 minutes. Bank coals at back of firebox. Make a drip pan of quilted broiling foil wider and longer than the roast. Place in front of coals to catch drippings. Put soaked hickory chips on coals. Place roast securely on motor-driven spit over coals. Use your smoker-hood to impart that hickory-smoked flavor to the meat, or fashion one of heavy foil. Cook roast 1 to 1½ hours, checking before 1 hour if your preference is for rare meat. ❧ Serve roast on wooden platter garnished with endive and pineapple rings sprinkled with fresh grated coconut. Accompany with wild rice seasoned with meat drippings.

6 TO 8 SERVINGS

NOTE: This is the center or "eye" of the rib roast with all bone, outside meat and fat removed. It is not rolled. This roast is often confused with the Spencer roast, which is the rib roast with bone removed, but not all outside meat. Spencer is much larger in diameter and fatter than the eye roast.

Roast on the Rocks

4-pound eye roast of beef,
   of uniform shape
2 cloves garlic, quartered
1 cup salt

4 tablespoons freshly ground black
   pepper
1 tablespoon ginger
Parsley
Quilted broiling foil

Remove roast from refrigerator well in advance of barbecue time, to reach room temperature before cooking. One hour before cooking, insert garlic quarters into well-spaced $1\frac{1}{2}$-inch-deep slits cut in meat. Blend salt, pepper, and ginger. Rub salt mix into meat, forcing as much as possible into all surfaces until roast is heavily coated. Just before cooking, remove garlic. ❧ Line grill firebox with quilted broiling foil. Add charcoal—enough to have a bed of coals 2 inches deep over entire area. Light and let burn until coals are hot and covered with gray ash. Roast is cooked directly on coals, relocated on fresh coals several times during cooking. Brush fine gray ash from surface of coals with folded newspaper. ❧ Place roast directly on coals. Cook for 10 minutes. Give roast one-third turn and relocate on fresh coals. Cook for 10 minutes. Roast will be charred on the surface, juicy-red inside. ❧ Toss 2 or 3 peeled garlic cloves into fire just before roast is ready to serve. ❧ Place roast on a wooden plank and garnish with parsley. Slice roast diagonally across the grain in $\frac{1}{8}$-inch slices.

4 SERVINGS

Roquefort Pocket Steak Avignon

3 pounds beef tenderloin (Cut from center of a whole tenderloin and left in 1 piece. If thicker than 1½ inches in places, have butcher flatten with cleaver to uniform 1½-inch thickness, then cut pocket in meat.)

MARINADE:

1¼ cups olive oil
¾ cup Burgundy
¼ cup fresh lemon juice
¼ cup soy sauce
3 cloves garlic, mashed
½ teaspoon dry mustard
½ teaspoon thyme
¼ cup celery leaves, chopped
1 Bermuda onion, chopped
Dash cayenne
Freshly ground pepper

STUFFING:

3 3-ounce packages genuine
  Roquefort cheese
¼ cup almonds, finely chopped
3 tablespoons ripe olives, chopped
2 tablespoons green olives, chopped
1 tablespoon parsley, minced
1 tablespoon green onion, minced
3 tablespoons truffles, chopped
  (or use mushroom stems)
2 dashes Tabasco sauce
2 teaspoons soft butter

FOR SERVING:

5 tablespoons soft butter
12 large fresh mushroom caps

1 package frozen peas
Nutmeg

Mix marinade ingredients and let meat soak in marinade for 2 hours at room temperature, turning occasionally. ?❧ Crumble Roquefort cheese into a bowl, add remaining stuffing ingredients and mix. Spoon stuffing into meat pocket and stitch opening with thread. Do not stuff too full. (Extra stuffing makes a delectable sandwich filling.) ?❧ Line firebox of grill with quilted foil, add charcoal and light, letting burn down until coals are gray. While fire is burning down, place mushroom caps with 3 tablespoons butter on sheet of foil and seal tightly with a double fold. Seal partially thawed peas with 2 tablespoons butter in foil also and place both on grill for about 15 to 20 minutes. When done but still crisp, place at side of grill to keep warm while cooking steak. You may also wrap a loaf of sour dough French bread spread with herb butter in foil and place on back of grate. ?❧ When charcoal has burned to gray coals, place wet hickory chips on coals. Place steak over coals and cover with a sheet of quilted foil, weighted down with rocks. Cook steak until done to your taste, turning and basting with marinade.

6 TO 8 SERVINGS

NOTE: *Serve steak on a large wooden platter surrounded with water cress. Slice some servings so stuffing shows. Place mushroom caps on water cress and fill each with peas. Dust with nutmeg. Arrange fresh flower blossoms between mushroom caps. If you wish to serve fewer persons, have pockets cut in individual servings of tenderloin, using half of marinade and stuffing recipes.*

Steak a la Arabia

2 pounds beef tenderloin
½ cup vegetable oil
1 large Bermuda onion, cut into
    wedges
2 green peppers, cut into strips
1 small can (2 ounces) pimientos,
    drained and chopped

2 cloves garlic
    Juice from 1 lemon
1 teaspoon salt
½ teaspoon pepper
    Quilted broiling foil

Make cooking pan by cutting a 14-inch square of quilted broiling foil, folding a double 1½-inch edge on all four sides, making diagonal folds at corners and bringing these corners back against the sides. ➺ Line firebox with foil and let fire burn down until coals are covered with gray ashes. ➺ Cut beef into strips about 2 inches long and ½ inch square. Set aside. ➺ In foil pan, cook onion and peppers in oil until slightly brown and tender. Add pimiento and meat; cook until slightly browned. Mash garlic; combine juice with lemon juice and add to meat mixture. Season with salt and pepper and cook 3 to 4 minutes longer.

4 SERVINGS

Filet Mignon Polynesian

4 beef tenderloin steaks (1½ inches
   thick—total weight about
   3 pounds)
1 cup corn oil
½ cup Worcestershire sauce
½ cup tarragon vinegar
½ cup lemon juice

1 8-ounce can tomato purée
3 cloves garlic, crushed
¼ cup butter
¼ cup grated Parmesan cheese
  Seasoning salt
1 fresh pineapple
  Quilted broiling foil

In a 2½-quart bowl, combine corn oil, Worcestershire sauce, tarragon vinegar, lemon juice, tomato purée and garlic. Flatten the steaks with a meat cleaver; place in marinating mixture for 40 minutes. ᗌ Line firebox of grill with foil. Add charcoal and light. Let burn until coals are covered with gray ash. ᗌ Remove steaks from marinade and pat dry with paper towels. Place on a sheet of foil and sprinkle with seasoning salt. Raise rack of grill about 4 inches above coals. Grill steaks on foil about 15 minutes; turn and top each with 1 tablespoon butter and 1 tablespoon Parmesan cheese; broil 15 minutes. ᗌ While waiting for meat to cook, peel and core pineapple. Slice off 4 rings. Place each on a square of foil. When steaks are done, place one on each pineapple slice and serve immediately.

4 SERVINGS

Beef Broil Beautiful

4-pound filet of beef, about 3 inches
   in diameter
3 tablespoons olive oil
1 tablespoon salt
1 tablespoon cracked black pepper

Quilted broiling foil

SAUCE:
¾ cup butter (1½ sticks)
¼ teaspoon cayenne pepper
¼ cup flour
 1 tablespoon parsley, finely chopped
 1 tablespoon tarragon leaves, finely
   chopped (or 1½ teaspoons
   crushed dried tarragon)
 1 cup dry white wine
   Juice of 1 lemon (about 3
   tablespoons)

Remove filet from refrigerator 1½ hours before cooking, and allow to come to room temperature. Rub well with olive oil, salt, and coarse black pepper. Wrap in foil, folding the top and ends over several times to seal completely. ᘓ Line firebox of grill with foil, add charcoal and light. Let burn until gray ashes cover coals. ᘓ Meanwhile make the sauce: Melt butter in saucepan, add cayenne, and blend in flour until smooth. Add parsley and tarragon, then gradually stir in wine and lemon juice. Stir constantly over low heat until smooth and thick. Keep warm on back of grill. ᘓ Place wrapped filet on grill-rack with firebox 4 to 5 inches from grill. Cook 22 to 25 minutes, turning every few minutes with a spatula so as not to pierce the foil seal. Remove from fire and carefully fold back foil. Lift out filet and place directly on grill. Pour juices into sauce. Brown filet quickly about 2 minutes on each side, remove to heated platter and allow to stand about 10 minutes before serving. Carve in 1-inch slices (or thinner if you prefer) and garnish with fresh parsley. Blend juices into sauce and pass separately to be spooned over filet.

6 GENEROUS SERVINGS

NOTE: This recipe makes lots of delicious, tart, rich sauce, somewhat like the classic Béarnaise, which is a bit tricky to make.

Ginger Steak Hawaiian

4 to 5 pounds 2-inch thick sirloin
   steak

GINGER MARINADE:

½ cup soy sauce
½ cup pineapple juice
 2 tablespoons ginger
 4 tablespoons sake or sherry
 1 tablespoon butter
 1 teaspoon dry mustard
 1 teaspoon garlic juice
½ teaspoon curry powder

TORCH BANANAS:

3 ripe bananas
1 tablespoon lemon juice
2 tablespoons pineapple juice
2 tablespoons melted butter
1 tablespoon honey
3 tablespoons shredded coconut

FLAME SAUCE:

4 tablespoons butter
3 tablespoons brandy or gin
  Quilted broiling foil

Trim steak of excess fat, reserving fat. Score fat edge of steak at 2-inch intervals. In a shallow dish, large enough to accommodate steak, combine all marinade ingredients; mix well. Place steak in marinade; refrigerate for 3 hours. Turn steak after marinating 1½ hours. ৽ Line brazier with quilted broiling foil. Add charcoal in one layer solid formation; light and let burn until white ash covers surface of coals. ৽ Peel bananas; cut in halves lengthwise. Brush with lemon juice. Cut three strips 10 inches long, of quilted broiling foil. Place 2 banana halves on each piece of foil, cupping edges of foil around bananas. Blend pineapple juice, melted butter and honey; brush bananas with this mixture. Sprinkle with coconut. Bring edges of foil together over bananas, fold with drugstore fold. Double fold ends toward center. ৽ Drain marinade from steak into a square of quilted broiling foil cupped in the shape of a small pan. Grease grate with reserved fat and place 4 inches above coals. Place banana packets on outer edges of grate. ৽ Grill steak *8 to 9 minutes on each side* for rare, *10 to 12 minutes on each side* for medium, by a timer. Using tongs, turn once. To test for doneness, slit near bone and note color. Brush steak once or twice with marinade, on each side. Just before ready to serve, heat marinade. In another "cupped" foil pan, heat Flame Sauce. (Do not allow sauce to boil over.) ৽ Place steak on heated platter, cut in diagonal slices. Arrange bananas on platter. Ignite Flame Sauce and pour over bananas. Serve heated marinade with steak.

6 SERVINGS

California Chuck Wagon Steak WITH CALIMEXI BASTE

Top sirloin beef steak, 1 inch thick   ½ cup softened butter
  (allow 12 oz. per person)   1 teaspoon garlic salt

Blend together softened butter and garlic salt. Spread on both sides of steak. Let stand at room temperature while making baste.

CALIMEXI BASTE:
  1 6-ounce can orange juice
  1 5½-ounce can tomato juice
  1 4½-ounce can minced ripe olives
  1 1½-ounce package raisins

1 tablespoon soy sauce
1 teaspoon paprika
1 teaspoon garlic salt
1 teaspoon garlic powder
¼ teaspoon cayenne pepper

In saucepan, thoroughly mix baste ingredients, *except ½ teaspoon of the garlic powder*. Simmer for 25 minutes, stirring occasionally. Stir in remaining ½ teaspoon garlic powder and simmer 20 minutes longer. ও Line firebox of grill with quilted broiling foil. Heap on briquets, light and let burn until flames have died down.

QUICK BAKED POTATOES: Boil scrubbed, unpeeled, baking-size potatoes until half done. Wrap each in quilted foil. Start baking potatoes on grill ½ hour before grilling steak. ও Brown steak quickly on both sides over hot coals, then raise the grill about 2 inches. Turn steak every 2 to 4 minutes until done as desired. Baste steak with Calimexi Baste each time before turning, pressing baste into steak with back of fork. ও Place steak on heated serving platter, and spoon some of the baste over before serving.

Steak Flambees

1 sirloin steak, 1 to 1½ inches thick
1 cup bourbon whiskey
¼ cup lime juice
2 tablespoons brown sugar

3 tablespoons melted butter
Salt
Pepper
¼ cup kirsch
Quilted broiling foil

Place steak in shallow pan or dish. Combine bourbon, lime juice and brown sugar. Pour over steak, cover and marinate for 1 hour. ❧ Line firebox with quilted broiling foil and prepare fire. When coals are covered with gray ashes, place the steak on greased rack. Add melted butter to remaining marinade; baste steak generously and continue to baste frequently during the grilling. When the steak is well-browned on the under side, turn over and season with salt and pepper. At the desired degree of doneness, place steak on heated platter; pour kirsch over and ignite for serving.

SUGGESTED ACCOMPANIMENTS: Sautéed mushrooms, cheese potato boats and tossed green salad.

4 SERVINGS

Hawaiian Steak Ambrosia

4 pounds center cut porterhouse
    steak, 1½ inches thick
3 fingers fresh ginger root
2 cloves garlic
2 cups soy sauce

2 tablespoons sugar
¼ cup bourbon whiskey or brandy
1 tablespoon monosodium glutamate
    Quilted broiling foil

Roll steak and tie firmly. Peel and finely chop ginger root and garlic. Combine with remaining ingredients. Pour over steak and marinate for 1 hour. ❧ Line firebox with quilted broiling foil. Prepare fire and let burn until gray ashes form on coals. ❧ Place steak on greased grill and cook to desired doneness, basting frequently with the marinade. Remove to heated platter, carve and serve.

3 TO 4 SERVINGS

Lido Isle Steak

1 butt beef tenderloin, about 2½-3 pounds	12 mushrooms sliced
3 tablespoons butter	½ cup brandy
1 small onion, diced	½ teaspoon tarragon

Sauté onions in butter until soft and brown, then add mushrooms, brandy, and tarragon. Simmer until mixture is thick. Make an incision in the beef tenderloin, cutting lengthwise and almost all the way through. Stuff with mixture, then close gap with foil and tie meat in 3 or 4 places. Put on spit and charcoal broil about 40 to 45 minutes for rare. Baste occasionally with a little more butter and about 1 tablespoon brandy.

FINES HERB FRENCH FRIES

2 packages frozen French fries	½ teaspoon fines herbs
Salt and pepper	Quilted foil

Place frozen potatoes in foil, add salt and pepper and fines herbs. Wrap in foil and place on grill, turning occasionally, until done, about 8 minutes.

4 SERVINGS

Barbecued Beef Head OLD CALIFORNIA STYLE

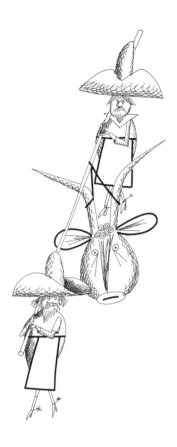

1 beef head with hide
 Wire and burlap
 Rocks or/and bricks
 Oak wood

Vinegar
Chopped parsley
Radish roses
Parsley sprigs

Make a pit, 3 feet by 3 feet by 3 feet, and line bottom and sides with bricks or/and rocks. Build and light a fire of oak wood. After fire has started, add more bricks or rocks to heat. ॐ Clean and trim the beef head, leaving hide on, and wrap well in quilted broiling foil. Make a wire sling with a handle, place sling around the foil-wrapped head, having the handle on top. ॐ When the fire has died down to embers, remove the surplus hot bricks or rocks, leaving those that were used for lining bottom and sides of pit. Also remove the hot coals, and set aside. ॐ Now place the prepared head in the pit with the handle on top. Cover it up with the surplus hot bricks or rocks and coals. Seal the pit with damp burlap, cover with dirt to hold heat in, making sure the handle of the wire sling is above ground. Leave overnight, or 8 to 12 hours, depending on size of head. ॐ When head is done, remove cover and head and unwrap. Cut away the hide, slice off the meat, and place on a large platter. Remove the tongue, slice and place on platter, garnishing both platters with radish roses and parsley sprigs. Remove brain, slice and serve on separate platter with vinegar and chopped parsley. Serve with buttered garlic French bread, Spanish Salsa, potato salad, carrot and celery sticks, cucumbers, olives, etc.

SPANISH SALSA:
 2 or 3 pounds green chili peppers
 1 pound onions

4 pounds fresh tomatoes,
 or 4 #2½ cans tomatoes, drained
4 teaspoons salt

Hold peppers over fire with fork or stick until skins are blistered. Wrap in damp cloth until cool; then peel off skins, remove stem end, slit open, and remove seeds. Chop peppers and onions in very small pieces in large bowl. Remove skins from tomatoes by holding over fire, chop, and add with salt to peppers and onions. If canned tomatoes are used, drain off juice and cut in small pieces. A little vinegar may be added if desired.

15 TO 20 SERVINGS

NOTE: *Here is real old western he-man fare! Though it may not appeal to all, we could not resist including this recipe, as it is an authentic and traditional old pioneer dish, still served at round-ups and stockmen's barbecues and considered a great delicacy. It takes a bit of doing to find a whole unskinned beef head unless you own your own ranch, but perhaps you can butter up someone who works in a packing house.*

Spiced Hawaiian Honey Steak

1 pound ground lean beef	1/16 teaspoon nutmeg
1 fresh pineapple	1 banana, sliced
¼ cup honey	4 maraschino cherries
¼ teaspoon cinnamon	4 green stuffed olives
¼ teaspoon paprika	1 bunch fresh parsley
⅛ teaspoon curry powder	Quilted broiling foil
⅛ teaspoon ginger	

Line firebox with quilted broiling foil. While coals are burning down, peel and core pineapple. Slice off 4 rings. ᓒ In a 1½-quart bowl, combine beef, honey and spices. Shape into 4 patties. Place patties and pineapple slices on a sheet of foil; place on grill and cook to desired doneness. ᓒ Remove steak patties to warm serving platter; top each with a grilled pineapple slice. Toothpick a cherry and an olive through the center of the pineapple slices. Surround with pieces of banana. Garnish with parsley. Serve hot.

4 SERVINGS

Zippy Roll

1½ pounds ground chuck roast
1 pound pork sausage
1 cup canned crushed pineapple
1 cup chopped dried apricots,
    loosely packed
4 tablespoons cognac
2 cups cooked rice

¾ cup coarsely chopped blanched
    almonds
2 eggs, separated
2 teaspoons chili powder
Endive
Spiced apples
Quilted broiling foil

Drain pineapple, reserving syrup. Add apricots and cognac to drained pineapple, let stand until apricots soften. Drain, adding "nectar" to reserved pineapple syrup. Add drained fruit and almonds to rice. ∂◆ Line firebox of grill with quilted broiling foil. Add briquets, light and let burn until flames have died down. ∂◆ Combine ground chuck, sausage, egg *yolks* and chili powder; mix thoroughly. Interlock and double-fold together 2 lengths of quilted broiling foil to make a strip measuring approximately 18 by 20 inches. Place meat mixture on foil and pat out into a rectangle about 12 by 14 inches. ∂◆ Beat egg whites until stiff. Fold into rice-fruit mixture. Spread on meat to within 1 inch on each end and to within 2 inches on "sealing side." Roll as jelly roll. Seal the side and fold in the ends. Place roll of meat in center of foil strip. Bring sides of foil together over roll and fold down the length of meat roll. Triple fold ends and press up against ends of roll. ∂◆ Place on a low grill over very hot coals. Turn to expose a new surface to heat every 5 minutes, for a total of 40 minutes. Raise grill and turn 4 more times at 5-minute intervals. Total cooking time 1 hour. ∂◆ Heat syrup mixture.

To Serve: Place roll on large platter. Unwrap and tuck foil down around roll. Surround with endive and spiced apples. Pour heated syrup over roll. May be flamed.

6 SERVINGS

Beef-Burger Main Line

MAIN LINE SAUCE:

3 medium-size onions, sliced
4 tablespoons butter
4 tablespoons beef extract
½ cup boiling water
½ cup sauterne wine
1 can tomatoes, drained
1 cup tomato catsup
1 4-ounce can mushrooms, diced
½ cup seedless raisins
½ cup diced macadamia nuts
1 cup diced green pepper
1 cup finely cut parsley

1 cup diced celery
1 tablespoon lemon juice
1 tablespoon dark brown sugar
1 teaspoon salt
1 teaspoon dry mustard
½ teaspoon coarse, freshly ground
   pepper
½ teaspoon celery seed
¼ teaspoon nutmeg
¼ teaspoon soy sauce
   Quilted broiling foil

In 3-quart aluminum saucepan, sauté onions in butter until tender and lightly browned. Dissolve beef extract in boiling water; add wine. Mix remaining ingredients in large bowl. Add to sautéed onions along with beef extract, wine mixture. Simmer on grill for 1 hour. 𝄞 Line firebox with quilted broiling foil. Add a heap of charcoal or briquets and light. Let burn until flames have died down.

BEEF-BURGER BALLS:

3 pounds freshly ground top round,
   ground twice
   Meat tenderizer
   Melted butter

Toasted, salted coconut chips,
   for garnish
Quilted broiling foil

Form 8 "beef-balls," slightly flatten tops and bottoms. Sprinkle lightly with meat tenderizer. Brush with melted butter. Brown about 6 inches above coals. Turn at frequent intervals. Finish cooking to desired doneness on a strip of quilted broiling foil. 𝄞 To serve, spoon Main Line Sauce over Beef-Burgers and sprinkle with coconut chips.

8 SERVINGS

59

Mexisirwine Roll

1½ pounds ground sirloin steak
⅓ cup Burgundy
4 slices day-old bread
½ cup evaporated milk
1 medium onion, minced
2 cloves garlic, minced
¼ cup butter
2 canned pimientos, slivered

1 cup green-ripe pitted olives, cut
 in quarters
3 egg yolks
2 egg whites, slightly beaten
½ teaspoon paprika
¼ teaspoon pepper
2⅛ teaspoons salt
Quilted broiling foil

Pour wine over meat; let stand. Break the bread into small pieces in a large mixing bowl; pour milk over it. Let stand. ࢢ Cook onions and garlic in butter for 2 minutes over low fire. Add all ingredients to the bread-and-milk mixture. Mix lightly but thoroughly. ࢢ Dust a 20-inch strip of quilted broiling foil with flour. Spoon meat mixture into center; form into a cylinder about 3 inches wide. Roll tightly in foil and twist one end tightly back of meat roll. Stand roll on end, allowing meat to settle into a compact roll. Twist other end of foil tightly. Repeat with a second piece of foil to assure a compact loaf. ࢢ Line firebox with quilted broiling foil. When coals are covered with a gray ash, place meat roll on grill. Bake for 20 minutes, turning 2 or 3 times. ࢢ Remove foil wrapper from meat and place directly on grill. Bake until golden brown, turning frequently and basting with Bar-B-Wine Sauce. Remove from grill and slice for serving.

BAR-B-WINE SAUCE: Combine ¼ cup Paisano wine, ¼ cup melted butter and ¼ cup Mexican pepitas (pumpkin seeds).

6 SERVINGS

Singapore Satays

Place 8 to 10 hickory chips in a can of water; cover tightly. One hour before cooking time, line a hibachi with quilted broiling foil. Add oak and briquets; light and let burn until there is a nice bed of coals without any flames. *Five minutes before cooking time*, place hickory chips on top of coals.

2 pounds of beef, cut in 1-inch cubes	green stick skewers meat tenderizer

Thread 3 cubes of beef on each skewer. Sprinkle lightly with meat tenderizer.

SAUCE:

½ cup grated coconut	2 tablespoons chili powder
½ cup evaporated milk	1 tablespoon lemon juice
½ cup water	1 tablespoon lime juice
⅓ cup peanut butter	2 teaspoons curry powder
1 small onion, quartered	1 teaspoon salt
1 clove garlic, quartered	2 dashes Angostura bitters
	4 tablespoons butter
	Quilted broiling foil

In a saucepan, combine coconut, milk and water. Bring to a boil. Remove from heat and cool. Pour into a blender, add remaining sauce ingredients, *except butter*, and beat to a smooth sauce. Pour into saucepan, add butter and heat, stirring constantly. Keep warm. ❧ Shield hibachi on windward side with quilted broiling foil folded lengthwise. Place skewered meat on hibachi and let smoke about 10 minutes. ❧ Serve with individual bowls of hot cooked rice and individual bowls of warm sauce so that each person may dip the meat into the sauce and lift it, dripping, across the rice, to eat.

4 SERVINGS

Barbecued Stroganoff

1 pound round steak, cut in ¾-inch cubes
1 10½-ounce can tomato soup
1 6-ounce can broiled mushrooms, drained
1 cup sour cream
½ cup chopped onion
1 clove garlic, minced

1 tablespoon Worcestershire sauce
6 - 8 drops Tabasco sauce
½ teaspoon salt
⅛ teaspoon pepper
4 large potatoes
Oil
Quilted broiling foil

Line outdoor grill with quilted foil to reflect radiant heat. Heap charcoal briquets in grill and light. Allow fire to burn for approximately 30 minutes, or until gray ash covers the briquets. ❧ Place cubes of steak on skewers. Brown over coals, turning to brown on all sides. ❧ Meanwhile, make sauce. In a bowl mix together soup, mushrooms, cream, onion, garlic, sauces, salt and pepper. ❧ Tear off 4 rectangles of quilted foil measuring approximately 9 by 14 inches. Remove steak from skewers and place one-quarter of meat on each piece of foil. Top with one-fourth of sauce. Close foil with drugstore fold across top and double fold ends toward center to seal. ❧ Scrub potatoes; rub with oil. Wrap tightly in quilted foil and place directly on top of coals. Place meat packets on grill about 4 inches above coals. After 35 minutes, turn potatoes on coals and gently turn meat packets. Continue cooking for 40 minutes.

To SERVE: Remove potatoes to individual plates. Slit foil, cross-cut potatoes and press gently to break open. Open one end of meat packets and slip Stroganoff onto potato. Garnish with parsley.

4 SERVINGS

Bedeviled Beef

3 pounds beef round
1 clove garlic, minced
2 tablespoons chopped parsley
2 tablespoons thyme
2 tablespoons grated lemon rind
1½ teaspoons salt

½ teaspoon pepper
1 3-ounce can grated Parmesan
    cheese
1 cup dry sherry wine
1 4½-ounce can deviled ham
Quilted broiling foil

Pound the beef with dull edge of a heavy knife, then cut in 2- or 3-inch squares. Place in shallow pan or dish. Combine garlic, parsley, thyme, lemon rind, salt, pepper, cheese and wine; pour over beef. Cover tightly with quilted foil. Marinate in refrigerator overnight. ও Cut six 7-inch squares of foil. Spread the center of each with deviled ham; place beef on top and seal securely. Refrigerate until time to grill. ও Line firebox with quilted foil. When coals are covered with gray ash, place packets of meat on grill and cook 10 to 12 minutes on each side. Serve immediately.

6 SERVINGS

Barbecued Honey Short Ribs Orientale

5 pounds lean short ribs of beef,
   cut in 2-inch lengths
½ cup sliced green onions
3 tablespoons soy sauce
3 tablespoons sherry or Burgundy
   wine
3 tablespoons honey
2 tablespoons lemon juice

2 teaspoons monosodium glutamate
1 teaspoon garlic salt
1 teaspoon pepper
1 teaspoon soda
½ teaspoon curry powder
½ teaspoon chili powder (optional)
   Quilted broiling foil

Score short ribs by criss-crossing meaty part of ribs with sharp knife—*being careful not to cut more than ¼-inch deep.* In a large kettle, mix thoroughly remaining food ingredients. Marinate the short ribs in this mixture overnight, stirring 2 or 3 times so that the flavor of the marinade penetrates the meat. Cut off a square of quilted broiling foil. Fold in half twice to form a smaller square. Triple-fold two sides to seal. Drain marinade from short ribs into packet. Triple-fold top to seal; freeze for future use. Line firebox of grill with quilted broiling foil. Add fuel, and light. Let burn until flames have died down. Brown ribs on grill about 5 minutes on each side. Wrap ribs in a double-thick strip of quilted foil. Place on grill and cook for about 15 or 20 minutes, turning 3 or 4 times.

6 SERVINGS

Lanai Barbecued English Ribs of Beef

2 selected English ribs of beef
    8 inches long, cut into 2 equal
    parts, to be served 1 to a person
½ cup wine vinegar
½ cup pineapple juice
 4 tablespoons papaya pulp
2 tablespoons dark brown sugar
2 tablespoons peanut or olive oil
2 tablespoons soy sauce
½ teaspoon cumin seed

½ teaspoon thyme
½ teaspoon salt
½ teaspoon paprika
¼ teaspoon black pepper
¼ teaspoon garlic powder
⅛ teaspoon oregano
⅛ teaspoon rosemary
 2 tablespoons honey
 1 cup grated pineapple
   Quilted broiling foil

In a saucepan, mix vinegar, pineapple juice, papaya, sugar and oil. Simmer, to bind and blend, then stir in soy sauce. Thoroughly mix herbs by rubbing them together. Add 1 *teaspoon* herb mixture to heated basting liquid. ❧ Score ribs and rub a generous amount of herb mixture into slashes. (Reserve remaining herbs.) Place ribs in refrigerator dish, cover with basting liquid. Marinate in refrigerator 6 to 8 hours, turning ribs occasionally. ❧ Line firebox of grill with quilted broiling foil. Add charcoal, light and let burn until coals are glowing. ❧ Remove ribs from marinade. Drain 5 minutes on paper towels. Add honey to marinade. Secure ribs in wire spit-rack. ❧ Rake coals slightly to back of spit area. Make a drip pan of broiling foil, 4 to 6 inches wide, 1½ inches deep and a little longer than the ribs in spit rack. Place in firebox in front of coals. Place spit in position for motor drive. As ribs revolve above coals, baste with marinade. As ribs begin to brown, sprinkle with ½ *teaspoon* of herb mixture. Cook for 45 minutes, or until tender. ❧ Place ribs on individual strips of quilted broiling foil. Mix remaining herbs and marinade into pineapple. Spoon onto ribs. Close foil over ribs, place on grate to simmer at least 15 minutes. Open foil and garnish ribs with finely cut parsley.

4 SERVINGS

Barbecued Berkshire

Whole piglet, 25 to 35 pounds
6 tablespoons salt
1 teaspoon pepper
1 teaspoon garlic salt
1 pound green onions, tops included
2 pounds apples
  Large red apple for garnish

BASTING SAUCE:
⅔ cups wine vinegar
⅔ cups lemon juice
⅔ cups salad oil
  3 garlic cloves, chopped
  1 teaspoon soy sauce
  1 teaspoon salt
¼ teaspoon freshly ground pepper

Buy whole, cleaned piglet from your butcher. (Arrangements should be made a week in advance for oven-ready piglet weighing 25 to 35 pounds.) ৼ Combine salt, pepper, and garlic salt and rub ⅔ of mixture into the cavity of the piglet, saving the remaining ⅓ for the outside. Stuff the cavity with the green onions and apples, which have been halved and cored but unpeeled. Using metal skewers, truss the cavity with heavy cord or wire. Place piglet on spit 6 feet long, fastening securely to spit with wire or cord wound criss-cross fashion around body of piglet. It is now ready to be placed on the grill. ৼ Start spit, making sure that spit turns in *front* of, not over, coals so that drippings will not drop on the fire. Use a drip pan to catch the fats while roasting. Baste periodically with basting sauce. Start testing piglet at the end of 3 hours, although it may take as long as 5 hours to cook well done. At serving time place large red apple in piglet's mouth. ৼ This charcoal broiled Berkshire is ideal for large groups and is certainly the epitome of festivity.

20 TO 30 SERVINGS

Pork Tenderloin Javanese

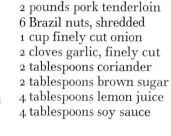

2 pounds pork tenderloin
6 Brazil nuts, shredded
1 cup finely cut onion
2 cloves garlic, finely cut
2 tablespoons coriander
2 tablespoons brown sugar
4 tablespoons lemon juice
4 tablespoons soy sauce

4 tablespoons olive oil
¼ teaspoon crushed red pepper or
    chili
Quilted broiling foil

GARNISH:
    Kumquats
    Fresh orange leaves

Line firebox of grill with quilted broiling foil. Add charcoal or briquets. Let burn until gray ashes cover coals and flames have subsided. ঈ Cut pork tenderloin in 1-inch cubes. In large bowl, mix nuts, onion, garlic, coriander, sugar, lemon juice, soy sauce, oil and pepper, until well blended. Add cubes of pork; marinate for 10 minutes. ঈ Place pork on skewers. Grill over coals about 10 minutes for each side. Baste with marinade once on each side. ঈ To serve: Slide pork cubes off skewers. Garnish with kumquats and orange leaves. Saffron rice, or lightly curried rice with currants, makes an excellent accompaniment.

4 SERVINGS

Indonesian Pork Saté

3 pounds pork loin, boned and cut
    into 1-inch cubes
¾ teaspoon salt
½ teaspoon pepper
1 tablespoon ground coriander
1 tablespoon cumin seed

1 cup onions, thinly sliced
1 tablespoon brown sugar
¼ cup soy sauce
1 teaspoon monosodium glutamate
    Dash ginger
¼ cup lemon or lime juice

Place pork cubes in shallow dish. Combine rest of ingredients and pour over cubes. Marinate overnight or at least 4 hours. Drain and save marinade. ?> Arrange 4 cubes per skewer, ¼ inch apart, and brush with marinade. Grill 5 minutes 3 inches from coals. Turn pork, baste with marinade, and grill another 5 minutes. Continue turning and basting every 5 minutes until pork is brown and well done on all sides, approximately 25 minutes in all.

6 SERVINGS

Indonesian Pork WITH PEANUT SAUCE

4 pork steaks, 8 ounces each,
  ½ inch thick
½ cup vinegar
¼ cup water
3 tablespoons soy sauce
2 teaspoons ground ginger

7 tablespoons brown sugar
Salt
¼ cup peanut butter
2 tablespoons brown sugar
1 tablespoon vinegar
2 tablespoons water
Quilted broiling foil

Line firebox with quilted broiling foil. Let coals burn down until covered with a gray ash. ❧ Place each steak on a 14-inch square of foil. Seal 3 sides by folding over 2 or 3 times (drug store wrap). Combine vinegar, water, soy sauce, ginger, brown sugar and salt. ❧ Pour ¼ of mixture into each packet of meat and seal fourth side of each. Let stand for 20 minutes. ❧ Place packets on grill and cook for 10 minutes on each side. Remove steaks from packets and place directly on grill. Cook until done, basting with sauce from packets. ❧ Remove to warm platter. Serve with peanut sauce.

PEANUT SAUCE: Combine peanut butter, brown sugar, vinegar and water. Set aside.

4 SERVINGS

Pork Polynesian Mariner

4-pound center-cut pork loin roast
   (have butcher cut backbone
   loose for easy carving)
1 teaspoon sage
  Salt
  Pepper
  Garlic salt

1 fresh coconut
2 tablespoons lime juice
2 tablespoons slivered almonds
1 No. 2 can pineapple chunks
3 bananas, split in half
1 7-ounce can minced clams
  Quilted broiling foil

Line firebox with foil. Let fire burn until gray ashes cover coals. ✌ Make a 4- to 5-inch cut in front of rib section of roast to form a pocket. Rub roast with sage, salt, pepper and garlic salt. Place roast on revolving barbecue spit and cook for 1¼ hours. ✌ Puncture coconut with an ice pick, drain off milk, and shred 2 tablespoons of the meat. Combine milk with lime juice and baste the roast with this mixture several times during cooking. ✌ In an aluminum broiling pan, combine 1 tablespoon of the grated coconut with almonds, pineapple and bananas. Remove roast from the spit and place on top of fruit mixture. Open pocket; pour in clams, clam juice, and any remaining basting mixture. Sprinkle with remainder of grated coconut. Cover with quilted broiling foil and place on grill. Cook for 45 minutes. ✌ Serve right in the broiler pan, garnished with unpeeled bananas, chunks of coconut meat, and endive or available greens.

4 TO 6 SERVINGS

Pacific Beach Stuffed Pork Chops

6 1½-inch thick pork chops
1 #211 buffet tall can crushed
   pineapple
½ cup brown sugar

1 teaspoon dry mustard
   Salt and pepper
3 tablespoons Cointreau
   Fresh, shredded coconut
   Quilted broiling foil

Line firebox of smoke cooker with quilted broiling foil. Add charcoal, light and let burn until flames have died down, and coals are medium hot. ले Drain syrup from pineapple into a bowl. Stir in brown sugar and mustard. Slit pork chops along fat edge to form stuffing pocket. Rub chops well with salt and pepper. Mix Cointreau into drained pineapple, stuff chops with this mixture. Close pockets with skewers. ले Add wet hickory chips to coals. Make a shallow pan of quilted broiling foil. Place chops in pan and brush with half the syrup mixture. Place in smoke cooker. Set smoke cooker for light smoke. Cook for 45 minutes. ले Turn chops in quilted foil pan, brush with remaining syrup mixture. Cook for an additional 45 minutes. Remove from cooker. ले Sprinkle chops with coconut and serve from quilted foil pan.

6 SERVINGS

Pork Orientale

2 pork tenderloins of equal size (total 1½-2 pounds)

STUFFING:	MARINADE:
1 cup dried mushrooms	¾ cup soy sauce
1 cup canned bamboo shoots	6 tablespoons sugar
¾ cup canned water chestnuts	6 tablespoons sherry
2 tablespoons green onions	½ teaspoon salt
¼ teaspoon monosodium glutamate	¼ teaspoon pepper
1 teaspoon soy sauce	½ teaspoon monosodium glutamate
2 tablespoons marinade	Quilted broiling foil

Line grill with foil. Add charcoal and light. Let burn until coals are covered with gray ashes. Combine all marinade ingredients and blend well. Split each pork tenderloin and flatten. Place in flat pan and cover with marinade for ¾ hour. ✌ Soak dried mushrooms in water for ½ hour. Dice mushrooms, bamboo shoots, water chestnuts and green onions. Place in bowl, add monosodium glutamate, soy sauce, marinade, and mix well. ✌ Take pork out of marinade and place one upon the other flat. Sew edges of three sides using heavy thread. Fill pocket completely with stuffing and sew remaining side tight. Place spit rod through stuffed tenderloin. To keep pork from slipping or tearing, place a holding fork on both ends of meat then tie meat securely to each fork with cord or heavy thread. Place spit rod on rotisserie and rotate. Barbecue pork till well done. (Figure 40 minutes per pound.) Baste occasionally with marinade. ✌ At serving time cut and remove threads. Spoon stuffing to one side of meat on platter. Place rice on other side of pork. Garnish with parsley and accompany with Chinese Snowpeas steamed over coals.

SNOWPEAS:	¼ teaspoon monosodium glutamate
	⅛ teaspoon salt
4 cups snow peas	1 teaspoon soy sauce
½ cup chicken stock	Extra stuffing from pork orientale
¼-inch square of ginger root	4 large dried mushrooms

Clean snow peas. In bowl place peas, chicken stock, mashed ginger root, monosodium glutamate, salt, soy sauce and extra stuffing. Mix well. Place ingredients in quilted foil bowl. Halve 4 large dried mushrooms after soaking for ½ hour in water and place on top. Seal "bowl" by bringing sides together, pinching tightly. Place on top of grill, cook for 10 minutes. May be barbecued on open grill, turning often.

4 SERVINGS

Beer Batter Porka

8 medium-size loin pork chops	1 teaspoon salt
¼ pound butter	¼ teaspoon pepper
2 oranges or tangerines	1 can beer
1 cup flour	Quilted broiling foil

Line firebox of grill with quilted broiling foil. Let fire burn until gray ashes cover coals. Fashion a large pan (about 14 by 10 inches) out of foil. Put butter in pan and melt on grill 2 inches above coals. ৯ Squeeze juice from oranges into 1½-quart bowl. Add flour, seasonings, and beer. Mix thoroughly. Dip pork chops in batter. Brown on both sides in the melted butter. ৯ Raise grill to 5 or 6 inches above coals. Place chops on grill and cook about 15 minutes on each side. Serve immediately, garnished with segments of oranges or tangerines.

4 TO 6 SERVINGS

Spit and Polish Pork Chops

3 pounds 1-inch thick loin pork
  chops
1 large white onion, thinly sliced
  Salt and pepper
3 red apples
3 oranges
  Quilted broiling foil

SAUCE:
½ cup apple jelly
4 tablespoons butter
4 tablespoons lemon juice
2 teaspoons prepared mustard
1 teaspoon cinnamon

Line brazier with quilted broiling foil. Add briquets and light. Let burn until flames have subsided. ᏺ Sprinkle chops and onion slices with salt and pepper. Alternating chops and onion slices, carefully weave onto spit, balancing well. Push together snugly with clamps. Cut unpeeled apples and oranges into thick wedges. Insert between chops, peel side out. Secure with wooden picks. ᏺ Form a square of 14-inch broiling foil into the shape of a 2-cup pan. Add jelly, butter, lemon juice, mustard and cinnamon. Heat to blend. Brush entire surface of meat and fruits with jelly sauce. ᏺ Rake coals slightly to back of spit area. Make a drip pan of quilted broiling foil, 4 to 6 inches wide, 1½ inches deep, and a little longer than the chops on the spit. Place in brazier under spit area. Adjust chops on spit about 4 inches from coals. Turn and baste frequently with sauce. Chops will be done in about 40 to 60 minutes.

4 TO 6 SERVINGS

East Indian Chutneyed Ribs

4 pounds country spareribs
1 No. 2 can pineapple chunks
½ cup cider (or pineapple) vinegar
¼ cup white corn syrup
1 8-ounce jar chutney

¼ cup molasses
¼ cup soy sauce
4 bananas
3 large oranges
Quilted broiling foil

Cut ribs into pieces, 2 ribs each, and place in shallow pan or dish. Combine ½ cup pineapple juice (from can of pineapple) with vinegar and corn syrup; pour over ribs. Cover tightly with foil and marinate for 24 hours. ᔐ Line firebox with quilted broiling foil. When coals have a gray ash coating, place ribs on grill. Combine molasses and soy sauce with ½ cup of the marinade and baste ribs frequently while grilling (about 15 minutes on each side). ᔐ Cut bananas into 1-inch chunks and oranges into wedges. Thread pieces of pineapple, bananas and oranges onto skewers. Grill until lightly browned, basting with same marinade as used on the ribs. ᔐ Just before removing from grill, pour half of chutney over ribs. Reserve remainder of chutney to use as garnish. Serve ribs and fruit on warm platter.

4 SERVINGS

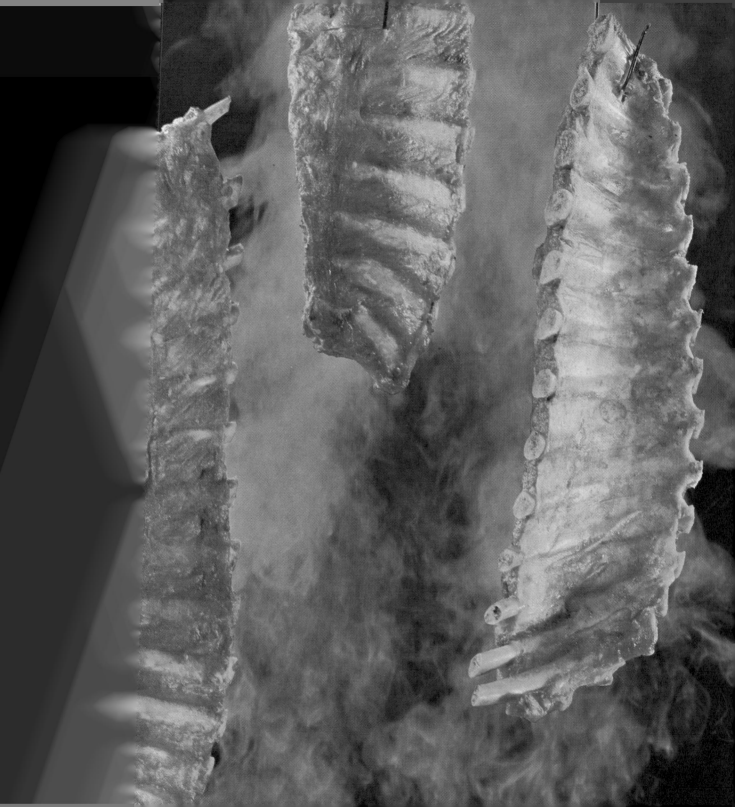

Ribs Regal

6 pounds spareribs (approximately 3 sides—purchase sides especially cut for
    barbecue, which have the fat bottom portion removed from the heavy end)

1 small onion, quartered
1 clove garlic, quartered
½ cup raisins
1 cup catsup
½ cup red wine (optional)
3 tablespoons brown sugar
2 tablespoons vinegar
1 tablespoon lemon juice
1 teaspoon dry mustard
1 teaspoon salt

½ teaspoon monosodium glutamate
½ teaspoon basil
¼ teaspoon black pepper
¼ teaspoon tarragon
¼ teaspoon rosemary
¼ teaspoon thyme
¼ teaspoon marjoram
⅓ cup butter
Quilted broiling foil

Place onion, garlic and raisins in blender. Grind finely. Add remaining sauce ingredients, *except butter*, blend well. Melt butter in saucepan; add blended mixture and simmer for 45 minutes, stirring often. (Any surplus sauce may be poured in a quilted foil packet, sealed, and frozen—ready for next cookout.) ᢙ One to two hours before barbecuing, place ribs on a strip of quilted broiling foil. Swab generously on all sides with sauce. ᢙ Ribs Regal are barbecued most successfully on a grill with hood and motor-driven spit. Line firebox of grill with quilted foil, about 30 minutes before cooking time. Pile briquets on foil; light and let burn until they are covered with gray ash. Move coals to the back of grill under hood. Make a drip pan of foil to catch the drippings from ribs as they cook: Form foil in pan-shape 4 to 6 inches wide, 1½ inches deep and a little longer than ribs on spit. Place in area over which ribs will turn. ᢙ Lace ribs on spit accordion fashion. Spread them over full length of spit to prevent crowding or overlapping. Run several metal skewers through ribs to hold securely. Attach spit to grill hood. When ribs are half-done (about 30 minutes), baste generously. Continue basting as ribs turn. Ribs are done when meat pulls away from bones. Cut in single-rib pieces and arrange in sunburst on round platter.

6 SERVINGS

NOTE: *Wrap ribs air-tight in quilted broiling foil and place in warming oven or near fire, to hold them at the peak of flavor, should serving time be delayed.*

Barbecued Spareribs and Prunes

1 full-length side of lean spareribs
  (not cracked, broken or cut, as
  rigid length is needed in making
  roll)
4 tablespoons mint jelly
1 ¾ cups sherry wine
4 tablespoons red wine vinegar
1 tablespoon orange peel
1 tablespoon lemon peel

1 tablespoon dry mustard
1 teaspoon allspice
15 - 20 tenderized prunes
15 whole cloves
2 cinnamon sticks
4 whole allspice
3 bay leaves
  Quilted broiling foil
  Length of fine wire

SAUCE: (May be made hours in advance, or just before using.) Melt jelly in saucepan. Add wine, vinegar, orange and lemon peel, mustard and the 1 teaspoon allspice. Remove from heat. Beat until well mixed. Add prunes so they may absorb spicy liquid. ౨ఴ Place ribs out flat and stick whole cloves in meat and fat. Lift fat layer and press prunes in under it, adding 2 half cinnamon sticks and 1 crushed bay leaf. Use remaining prunes to cover center portion of rib side, adding second halved cinnamon stick and crushed bay leaf. Dot with whole allspice. Brush sauce under flap, over prunes and exposed meat. Roll ribs, basting underside of ribs as they go into roll. Make a tight roll for ease of handling on spit or grill. ౨ఴ Tie roll securely with length of fine wire, wrapping around and around. Stuff open spaces at ends of roll with quilted foil. Baste entire roll. Insert spit and place prongs into meat. Place meat thermometer in thickest end without touching bone. ౨ఴ Line firebox with quilted broiling foil. Heap fuel in center, light and let burn until flames die down. Rake coals slightly to rear of spit. Place a drip pan of quilted foil under meat (4 to 6 inches wide, 1½ inches deep and longer than the roll on the spit). ౨ఴ Place meat quite high above coals, adjusting height to control browning. (Add fuel sparingly, as needed.) ౨ఴ Baste frequently with sauce—if not enough, finish basting with sherry. Roll requires 2¾ to 3 hours on spit (thermometer will register 185°). If cooked on grill, allow another 15 minutes. ౨ఴ To serve, cut wire, unroll, carve ribs. Serve with prunes.

2 SERVINGS

Ham Mandarin

1 slice tenderized ham, center cut, 1 inch thick
1 11-ounce can mandarin oranges
½ cup port wine
½ cup plum jam
3 tablespoons red wine vinegar
½ teaspoon kitchen bouquet
3 tablespoons grated orange rind
2 tablespoons cornstarch
½ teaspoon allspice
½ teaspoon dry mustard
Quilted broiling foil

Drain mandarin oranges. Combine juice, port wine, plum jam, vinegar, kitchen bouquet, grated orange rind, cornstarch, allspice, and dry mustard in electric blender. Blend thoroughly, then pour into 1½-quart saucepan. Simmer over medium heat, stirring occasionally, until reduced to half the original amount. Remove from heat. Chill thoroughly. ❧ Line firebox with quilted broiling foil. While coals are burning down to a gray ash, prepare Corn Rosemary.

CORN ROSEMARY: Cut 4 large squares of quilted broiling foil. On each, place 1 ear of corn spread with 1½ tablespoons soft butter and sprinkled with ⅛ teaspoon powdered rosemary, pinch of thyme, salt and pepper. Wrap each ear securely and grill for about 20 minutes. ❧ Trim all fat and rind from ham; place on sheet of foil three times the size of the ham. Spread sauce over ham and decorate with orange segments. Fold the ends of the foil over each other, sealing the package tightly. Place top-side down, on the grill over coals that have burned down to gray ashes. Cook for 10 minutes, turn the package over and cook an additional 20 minutes. ❧ Remove to warm serving platter and unfold foil for serving, being careful not to disturb the orange garnish. Serve with Corn Rosemary.

4 SERVINGS

Diamond Head Ham-n-Yam Volcanoes

4 ½-inch thick slices ham
4 yams (chubby, to resemble
   volcanoes)
4 large slices pineapple
   Quilted broiling foil

DIAMOND HEAD SAUCE:
½ cup margarine
½ cup syrup from pineapple
 4 tablespoons brown sugar
 1 tablespoon lemon juice
½ teaspoon dry mustard
¼ teaspoon ginger
¼ teaspoon cloves
 4 teaspoons brandy

Line firebox of grill with quilted broiling foil. Add charcoal, light and let burn until coals are covered with a fine gray ash. ❧ Remove small center bone from ham slices. Score fat. Brown slowly on grill over hot coals, turning frequently. ❧ While ham slices are browning, wash yams. Place on a large double-thick strip of 14-inch broiling foil. Cup the edges up around the yams. Add *2 cups boiling water*. Seal edges together carefully. Steam over fire. ❧ Form quilted foil in the shape of a 2-cup pan. Add margarine; melt over grill. Add pineapple syrup, sugar, lemon juice, mustard, ginger and cloves; stir to mix. ❧ Fold in half four strips of broiling foil 28 inches long. On each square, place one slice of browned ham. Add a small amount of sauce, then place a slice of pineapple on each side of ham. Remove yams from fire; open foil carefully; slide skins off yams. Cut a thin slice from wide end to make a firm base. Place a yam on each slice of pineapple, small end up. Make a "crater" in the top of yams, pricking the inside with a fork so sauce will penetrate yam. Spoon remaining sauce into "craters" and over yams. Draw edges of foil up carefully and seal. Place upright on grate, at least 10 inches above coals. Cook for ½ hour. ❧ Remove from fire; open foil carefully. When cool enough to handle, roll edges of foil into plate shape, crimping edges. Spoon 1 teaspoon brandy into each "crater." Just before serving, light brandy.

4 SERVINGS

Jamaica Ham

2 pounds ham steak 1 to 1½ inches thick
4 slices pineapple
½ cup maple syrup
4 tablespoons rum
4 tablespoons syrup from pineapple
Olive or salad oil
2 cooked potatoes
Seasoning salt
Quilted broiling foil

Score edge of ham at 2-inch intervals. Place pineapple slices on a square of quilted foil, folding edges up forming a double 1½-inch side on all four sides. Make diagonal folds at corners, folding triangular point against sides to form pan. Combine maple syrup, rum and pineapple syrup. Pour over pineapple. ❧ Line firebox of grill with broiling foil. Add briquets, light and let burn until flame dies down. ❧ Heat oil in skillet on grill. Slice and add potatoes, season with seasoning salt. Turn potatoes occasionally with spoon. ❧ Grill ham steaks about 5 to 6 inches above coals. Turn and baste with syrup mixture on pineapple every 5 minutes. Cook about a total of 40 minutes. ❧ Place pineapple slices on ham during last 5 minutes of cooking time. Pour remaining syrup mixture over potatoes.

4 SERVINGS

Roberto's Ham Steak

2 slices ham steak, about ½ inch
  thick
½ cup dry sherry wine
½ cup fresh grated coconut
1 small orange, peeled and sliced
1 tablespoon chopped fresh cilantro
  (Chinese parsley)

¼ cup melted butter
¼ cup honey
1 teaspoon finely chopped fresh
  ginger or crystallized ginger
Grated rind of the orange

Moisten surfaces of ham liberally with sherry. Cover one steak with grated coconut, the orange slices and chopped cilantro. Cover with second ham slice and fasten together with toothpicks. Combine remaining sherry, honey, ginger and orange rind and spread generously on both sides of filled ham steak. Place on grill about 6 to 10 inches above hot coals. Slow cooking allows the flavors in the filling to penetrate the ham—so don't rush it. Cook 12 to 15 minutes on first side, brushing with marinade several times. Using a broad turner or spatula, turn carefully and cook 12 to 15 minutes longer. It should be browned, the fat edges charred.

6 SERVINGS

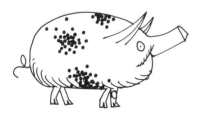

Roast Lamb Crème de Menthe WITH BUTTERMILK RICE

1 leg of lamb, boned, 5 to 6 pounds
1 package frozen chopped spinach
½ cup parsley, chopped
½ cup celery, finely chopped
½ cup lemon juice
1 tablespoon dry white wine
½ teaspoon salt
⅛ teaspoon pepper
¼ teaspoon garlic powder
18 fresh mint leaves
3 tablespoons crème de menthe
     liqueur
½ cup peanut oil

BUTTERMILK RICE:

1½ cups cooked rice
½ cup corn meal
3 cups buttermilk (do not use
     powdered)
¾ teaspoon soda
1 teaspoon salt
3 eggs
3 tablespoons melted butter
   Quilted broiling foil

Remove all "fell" (tissue-like covering) from lamb. Thaw spinach and mix next 7 ingredients, using only *1 tablespoon* of the lemon juice specified. Add 8 or 9 of the mint leaves, chopped. Spread stuffing mixture on lamb and roll up, tying every 2 inches with stout string. With a sharp knife make small incisions in lamb and insert rest of mint leaves. Rub in some salt. Place lamb securely on rotisserie over medium coals. For well-done lamb, allow about 2½ hours. If using meat thermometer, it should register 180° F. for well done, 140° or 150° if you prefer your lamb on the rare side. During last 15 minutes of cooking baste roast with mixture of remaining lemon juice, crème de menthe, and oil. Remove to hot platter and let set 10 minutes before carving. Drizzle about 1 teaspoon of any left-over crème de menthe mixture on each slice. ⅔ While lamb is cooking mix rice ingredients in order given in large bowl. Cut 8 squares of foil in 12-inch squares. Place a square of foil in a small bowl, patting it into shape of bowl. Place a serving of rice mixture in foil and seal tightly. Repeat until all is used, place foil packages on low-heat part of grill. Cook until slightly firm, moving packages about occasionally. Fold back foil and use as individual serving dishes. Decorate platter with shiny green leaves and white or cream colored blossoms.   8 SERVINGS

Boned Lamb New Orleans

5-pound boned leg of lamb (flat)
1 cup bourbon whiskey
¼ cup olive oil
1 clove garlic

1 pinch thyme
¼ teaspoon tarragon
¼ teaspoon rosemary

Rub lamb completely with garlic, then marinate 6 to 8 hours in well blended mixture of bourbon, olive oil, thyme, tarragon and rosemary. Line firebox of grill with quilted foil. Build charcoal fire and burn until coals are covered by the gray ash and flames have subsided. Barbecue approximately 45 minutes 6 to 8 inches from coals, turning and basting with marinade every 10 minutes. Slice in thin strips, garnished with mint leaves. Serve with fruit cocktail, rice, and French cut green beans.

6 SERVINGS

Lamb Julep

2 pounds lamb shoulder	2 teaspoons sugar
2 medium-size green peppers	6 tablespoons bourbon whiskey
½ cup mint sprigs	Quilted broiling foil

Line firebox with quilted broiling foil. While the fire is burning down, cut the lamb into 1-inch squares and the green peppers into large pieces. Thread the lamb and green peppers alternately onto skewers. ❧ Grill over hot coals, turning often. Muddle the mint sprigs, sugar and bourbon together. Just before removing skewers from the grill, baste with the bourbon mixture and ignite for serving.

4 SERVINGS

Lemon Butter Lamb Sirloin Steaks

8 lamb steaks, 1 inch thick
½ cup soft butter
½ teaspoon salt

2 tablespoons chopped parsley
2 tablespoons lemon juice
Tabasco sauce

Line firebox of grill with quilted broiling foil, arrange charcoal and light. Allow to burn for about ½ hour, or until gray ashes cover coals. ৯ Rub grill with piece of lamb fat, place steaks on grill, and cook 8 minutes on each side. Cut alongside of bone with sharp knife to determine when steaks are cooked to your liking. Most people prefer them when the inside is a very light pink. ৯ While charcoal is burning to desired cooking state, prepare lemon butter. Work softened butter in a bowl until creamy. Add salt, dash or two of Tabasco sauce and parsley. Slowly add lemon juice and blend. ৯ Top the steaks with the lemon butter and serve immediately on hot plates. Should serving be delayed, place cooked steak in foil at edge of grill. ৯ Mixed vegetables heated in a skillet on the grill make a tasty complement.

8 SERVINGS

Lambchops for Grandma WHO LIKES MARTINIS

10 small loin lambchops
  Salt
  Coarsely ground pepper
  Monosodium glutamate
½ teaspoon chopped parsley
 1 teaspoon chopped celery
 1 teaspoon chopped green pepper
  Pinch of rosemary
  Pinch of thyme
 1 cup gin

 1 cup vermouth
 8 shallots, minced
¼ teaspoon tarragon
 1 10-ounce can mushroom gravy
 1 3-ounce can chopped mushrooms
 1 cup port wine
½ cup coffee cream
½ cup butter
¼ teaspoon curry powder
 2 chili teppins

Line firebox with quilted broiling foil; let coals burn down until covered with gray ashes. ❧ Remove excess fat and skin from chops. Season with salt, pepper and monosodium glutamate. ❧ Place parsley, celery, green pepper, rosemary and thyme in a square of cheesecloth; bring edges together and tie securely. ❧ In a large bowl, combine gin, vermouth, shallots, tarragon and the cheesecloth packet of seasonings. Place lambchops in this marinade. ❧ In aluminum foil pan, combine mushroom gravy, mushrooms, wine and cream. Place at side of grill to cook slowly; stir occasionally to prevent sticking. ❧ In aluminum foil pan, melt butter; add curry powder and chili teppins. Push to back of grill. Make Instant Potato Purée. ❧ Remove lambchops from marinade. Dip both sides in butter mixture and grill, basting frequently with marinade. When chops are done (about 12 minutes on each side), remove to warm serving platter and serve with hot mushroom sauce.

INSTANT POTATO PURÉE: In large bowl, combine 3 cups boiling water, 1 cup cream, ¼ cup butter, 1 teaspoon salt. Stir in 1 package instant (flake form) mashed potatoes. When liquid is absorbed, whip lightly with fork. Add 1 cup cream, 1 cup full strength canned consommé, ½ cup grated Swiss cheese, 1 teaspoon chopped parsley, nutmeg and pepper to taste. Whip until combined. Spread in quilted foil pan; grill over coals while browning chops.
5 SERVINGS

Stuffed Lamb Patties Mozarella

2 pounds ground lamb
2 egg whites
¼ cup cracker meal
2 cloves garlic
1 8-ounce package Mozarella cheese, grated
2 egg yolks

¼ cup cracker meal
¼ cup chopped fresh mint leaves
8 teaspoons crème de menthe
Salt
Pepper
Quilted broiling foil

Line firebox of grill with foil. Let coals burn down until covered with a gray ash. ≥ Combine meat, egg whites and ¼ cup cracker meal in a 2½-quart bowl. Put the garlic through a press and add juice to the mixture. Mix thoroughly, form into 16 equal patties and make a depression in center of each. (An ice cream scoop may be used for this.) ≥ On a square of foil, combine cheese, egg yolks, ¼ cup cracker meal and mint leaves. Mix well and shape into 8 balls. ≥ Place a cheese ball on a patty, cover with a second patty, and roll into a ball. Wrap each in a double thickness of foil. Place on grill and cook for 25 to 30 minutes, turning frequently. ≥ Remove to warm serving platter and fold edges of foil down to form a saucer; sprinkle patties with salt and pepper, and spoon 1 teaspoon crème de menthe over each. Serve immediately.

8 SERVINGS

Veal Paprika Chops

4 veal chops, 1 inch thick

MARINADE:
⅓ cup sauterne
⅓ cup oil
1 tablespoon lime juice
1 tablespoon crushed juniper berries
1 small onion, grated
½ teaspoon paprika
Pinch garlic powder

TOPPING:
½ cup sour cream
1 tablespoon chives or parsley,
    chopped
Paprika
Quilted broiling foil

Combine marinade ingredients, pour over chops, and refrigerate several hours or overnight. ⅌ Line firebox of grill with quilted foil, add charcoal, light, and let burn until flames die down. ⅌ Drain chops. Place on grill and sear near coals. Salt to taste and remove to higher position. Turn and baste frequently until tender, about 35 minutes. ⅌ Remove from grill and top chops with mixture of sour cream and chives. Sprinkle with paprika and serve with baked potatoes.

4 SERVINGS

NOTE: If juniper berries are difficult to find, try the Health Food stores.

Breast of Chicken, Khmer, Flambée

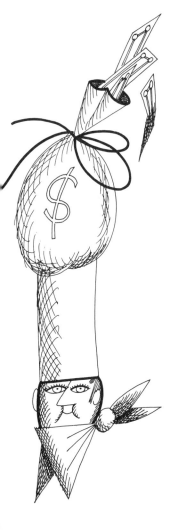

4 chicken breasts
¼ cup flour
1 teaspoon salt
½ teaspoon freshly ground pepper
1 egg, slightly beaten
½ cup finely ground cashew nuts
  (¼-pound)
1 teaspoon freshly grated nutmeg
4 green onions, minced
6 sprigs parsley, minced
¼ cup butter

1 13½-ounce can pineapple chunks
¼ cup chopped blanched almonds
¼ cup butter
3 tablespoons brown sugar
¼ cup white vinegar
½ cup preserved kumquats,
  not drained
2 tablespoons arrowroot or
  cornstarch
6 tablespoons (3 ounces) brandy
Quilted broiling foil

Blend flour, salt and pepper. Dip chicken breasts in flour mixture, then in egg and cover with cashews. Dust lightly with nutmeg. Place each on a large square of quilted broiling foil; top with minced onion, parsley and butter. Wrap each tightly, folding ends of foil to seal completely. ও Line firebox with quilted broiling foil. When the coals are covered with gray ashes, place packages of chicken on grill, approximately 3 inches above coals. Turn several times during cooking period (about 35 minutes). ও While the chicken is cooking, prepare Almond-Pineapple Sauce. Drain pineapple and reserve juice. In small aluminum-foil pan, cook almonds and pineapple chunks in butter until they are slightly brown. Blend in brown sugar, vinegar and kumquats. Make a paste of ½ cup pineapple juice and arrowroot; stir into sauce. Cook until slightly thickened. Move to back of grill to keep warm. ও When chicken is cooked, arrange on warm platter with Rice Bayon. Heat brandy, ignite and pour over chicken.

RICE BAYON: In top of double boiler, combine ¾ cup long-grain rice, 2 tablespoons vegetable oil, ¼ cup seedless raisins, ½ teaspoon tumeric, ½ teaspoon curry powder and ½ teaspoon salt. Stir well; add 1½ cups boiling chicken stock or bouillon. Cover and place over boiling water. Cook 20 minutes, or until rice is well done. Press into muffin pans or custard cups; unmold and arrange on warm serving platter with chicken. Serve at once with accompanying Almond-Pineapple Sauce.

4 SERVINGS

93

Breast of Chicken Vermouth

6 whole breasts of chicken (from 2½-pound broilers)

BRUSHING SAUCE:	VERMOUTH SAUCE:
¼ cup butter	¼ cup butter
¼ cup olive oil	1 cup sweet vermouth
¼ teaspoon Tabasco sauce	4 dashes Angostura bitters
¼ teaspoon seasoning salt	2 teaspoons grated orange rind
Juice of ½ lemon	½ teaspoon paprika

12 fresh pineapple sticks (3 inches long by 1 inch square)
½ cup Cointreau
¼ cup parsley, finely chopped
Quilted broiling foil

Bone and split the chicken breasts, making 12 filets. (Wings and trimmings can be used for broth.) ❧ For Brushing Sauce, melt butter in saucepan, add oil, Tabasco, salt and lemon. Mix and heat lightly. Do the same to make the Vermouth Sauce, adding other ingredients to melted butter and heating slightly. Keep both sauces warm. ❧ Line firebox of outdoor grill with foil, light charcoal, and bring to a steady gray-hot heat stage. Cover grill with a double thickness of quilted broiling foil. ❧ Brush both sides of filets with Brushing Sauce and place skin side down on foil-covered grill. Baste with remainder of sauce. Broil until brown on one side, baste with the Vermouth Sauce, turn, and finish cooking, basting with Vermouth Sauce and turning as needed. Broiling takes 20 to 25 minutes. ❧ Serve remaining Vermouth Sauce with breasts. Garnish with pineapple sticks which have marinated in Cointreau for 1 hour. Sprinkle with chopped parsley.

6 SERVINGS

Chicken Breasts Flamenco

6 chicken breasts
⅛ pound butter
¼ cup chopped parsley
¼ cup chives (or green onions),
    chopped

1 teaspoon dried basil
Butter for brushing
Heavy cream for brushing
Salt and pepper

Make small pockets in the chicken breasts, using a thin-bladed knife. Make a paste of the ⅛ pound of butter, parsley, chives and basil. Stuff the chicken breasts with this mixture and secure the openings with toothpicks or small skewers. Brush the breasts with butter and broil for 10 to 12 minutes, starting on the bone side and finishing skin side down. Just before they are done, brush with heavy cream and sprinkle with salt and pepper.

6 SERVINGS

Barbecued Chicken with Pacifica Marinade

12 meaty chicken breasts, or 6 fryers, halved

1½ cups pineapple juice	⅛ teaspoon marjoram
½ cup pale dry sherry	12 mushrooms
½ cup sauterne	1 bay leaf
1 teaspoon ginger	Parsley, green and red sweet
¼ teaspoon salt	pepper
⅛ teaspoon garlic powder	Quilted broiling foil

In large shallow bowl, mix pineapple juice, sherry, sauterne, ginger, salt, garlic powder, marjoram and bay leaf. Add chicken, place in refrigerator for 48 hours. Turn chicken 4 times daily. (For rapid cookout: Marinate 4 hours at warm room temperature, turning chicken frequently.) ✺ Line brazier with quilted broiling foil. Heap charcoal onto center of foil. Light and let burn down until flames have died. Spread coals to allow about ½-inch space between each adjacent coal. ✺ Remove chicken from marinade; drain. Cup a double-thick square of quilted broiling foil. Pour marinade into foil cup. Slice and add mushroom stems. Let simmer on edge of brazier until of thin syrup consistency. Simmer mushroom tops, cap down, 8 minutes. ✺ Place chicken on barbecue grill, skin side up. Cook breasts about 15 minutes on each side (halves about 18 minutes on each side). Turn chicken after 15 minutes (or half time), brush generously with marinade syrup. Repeat in 15 minutes. Raise grill to continue glazing but prevent burning. Turn and baste lavishly, twice again, cooking chicken about 2 minutes and 1 minute, respectively. Remove to heated platter. Place mushrooms, caps up, on chicken. Garnish with ⅛-inch strips of green and red pepper.

6 SERVINGS

Sam's Tonto Rim Chicken

4 chicken breasts
4 chicken thighs
½ cup salad oil
3 cloves garlic, thinly sliced
2 cups cracked wheat
3 chicken bouillon cubes

3 cups hot water
3 tablespoons soy sauce
1 cup sour cream
Roasting ears of corn
Quilted broiling foil

Line grill firebox with quilted broiling foil. Add briquets, light and let burn until flames die down. ❧ In a large skillet, place oil, garlic and cracked wheat. Sauté over hot coals until wheat is golden brown. Dissolve bouillon cubes in hot water, add soy sauce. Stir into wheat; mix thoroughly. Place chicken on top of wheat; cover and cook 30 minutes. (Liquid will be absorbed and wheat will be fluffy.) ❧ Remove skillet from grate. Place wet mesquite, oak or hickory chips on gray coals. Remove chicken from skillet and place skin side up on grate. Cover chicken with a strip of quilted foil, placing a few rocks along edges to hold foil in place. During the smoke-cooking of the chicken, lift the foil and turn chicken occasionally; replace foil. Cook chicken until tender and brown. ❧ Husk and wrap corn in quilted broiling foil. Place on grate with chicken and roast, turning occasionally, for about 20 minutes. ❧ While chicken is smoke-cooking, stir sour cream into wheat. Mix well, cover and set aside to keep warm.

4 SERVINGS

Foil-Wrapped Chicken Chinese

2 whole breasts of chicken or
   1 breast and 2 thighs
2 cloves garlic, crushed or finely cut
1 tablespoon minced fresh ginger (or
   chopped preserved ginger)
1 teaspoon salt
1 teaspoon chopped parsley

1 tablespoon honey
2 tablespoons olive oil
2 tablespoons sherry
2 tablespoons plum sauce (from
   Chinese store)
½ cup soy sauce
   Quilted foil

Bone chicken with sharp knife and cut into pieces about 1 inch wide and 1½ inches long. You should get 20 to 24 pieces from the whole chicken breast, about 6 to 8 from the thigh. Mix all sauce ingredients in large bowl, add chicken and marinate 30 minutes or longer. ᥤ Place each piece of chicken on a square of quilted foil, cut 7 by 7 inches, add a little marinade, and wrap each package securely, folding envelope fashion. Grill over hot coals about 7 minutes each side. Serve in foil wrappers, letting each guest unwrap his own. This makes about 3 to 4 dozen small bites, perfect for appetizers. To serve as an entrée, use whole chicken parts, boned or not as you like. Marinate and wrap as above, using 14-inch squares of foil. Grill about 12 to 15 minutes on each side.

4 TO 6 SERVINGS

Persian Chicken Pilaf

6 chicken thighs
¼ cup melted butter
1 teaspoon salt
1 cup instant rice
2 tablespoons dehydrated sweet
   peppers
3 tablespoons dehydrated onions
¼ cup seedless raisins

½ teaspoon tumeric
2 teaspoons granulated chicken
   bouillon
1 15-ounce can chicken broth
¼ cup bacon fat
1 3-ounce can sliced mushrooms
   Quilted broiling foil

Line firebox of grill with foil. Let coals burn down until covered with gray ash. ᘒ Wash chicken thighs and pat dry with paper towels. Brush each thigh with butter and sprinkle with salt. Place on grill and cook until golden brown, frequently turning and brushing with butter. ᘒ While chicken is cooking, combine rice, sweet peppers, onions, raisins, tumeric and bouillon in bottom of an aluminum foil pan; stir to blend evenly. ᘒ Combine chicken broth and bacon fat; pour over dry mixture in foil pan. Add mushrooms and juice. When chicken thighs are brown and tender, place on top of mixture and salt lightly. Cover pan with foil, seal sides and place on grill. Cook until liquid is absorbed by rice (approximately 20 minutes). Serve hot.

3 TO 4 SERVINGS

Tahitian Chicken Gauguin

4 2- to 2½-pound chickens; split in half lengthwise, joints broken, wings and legs skewered to bodies
1 large onion, diced
1½ cups butter
3 large tomatoes
½ cup lemon juice
½ cup lime juice
½ cup sauterne wine
2 teaspoons salt
½ teaspoon freshly ground pepper
1 fresh pineapple
1 cup chicken broth
8 bananas
½ cup Madeira wine
Quilted broiling foil

Early in the day, sauté onion in 3 tablespoons of the butter until golden. Peel, seed and dice tomatoes. Combine tomatoes and onion; purée in blender. Chill. ⮞ Mix lemon and lime juice, sauterne, salt, and pepper. Pour over chicken; marinate 1½ hours, turning chicken several times. ⮞ Line firebox of grill with quilted broiling foil. Add charcoal or briquets. Light and let burn until flames have died down. ⮞ Slice top from pineapple and set aside. Pare and core pineapple; cut into small chunks. Spread in the center of a large double-thick strip of quilted broiling foil. Dot with 1 tablespoon of the butter. Cup edges of foil, then pour chilled purée and chicken broth over pineapple. Fold ends of foil over top, leaving a small vent for steam to escape. Fold edges over to seal. ⮞ Melt remaining 1¼ cups of butter. Remove chicken from marinade; brush with butter. Adjust grill 7 inches above coals. Place chicken, skin side up, on grill. Baste with butter and turn at intervals. Place pineapple packet on "cool" side of grill to heat slowly and simmer gently. ⮞ After 1 hour, remove liquid from foil packet with meat baster. Add to any remaining melted butter. Peel bananas, cut in small chunks and place in packet. Add Madeira; heat to simmer point. ⮞ Dribble hot liquid and melted butter over chicken. Cook 15 minutes longer, turning and basting constantly. ⮞ To serve: Place pineapple top in center of large heated platter and surround with the chicken. Spoon heated fruit mixture over chicken.

8 SERVINGS

Barbecued Cardinal Chicken and Rice

1 frying chicken
1 cup tomato catsup
2 tablespoons sugar
3 tablespoons oil
1 tablespoon prepared mustard
1 tablespoon lemon juice

2 dashes Worcestershire sauce
2 dashes Tabasco sauce
Pepper
Garlic salt
Poultry seasoning
White vinegar

Cut chicken into serving pieces, leaving thighs attached to legs. ⇘ In large bowl, mix catsup, sugar, oil, mustard, lemon juice and sauces. Season to taste with pepper, garlic salt and poultry seasoning. Thin slightly with vinegar. Marinate chicken for 1 hour before cooking. ⇘ Line brazier with quilted broiling foil. Place charcoal on foil one layer deep and one-half inch apart. Light and allow to burn for about 1 hour for low, steady heat. ⇘ Place brazier rack on highest level over coals. Place chicken on rack, skin side up. Baste with marinade every 15 minutes. Cook slowly for about one-half hour. Turn chicken and, continuing basting, cook another half hour, or until done. ⇘ Prepare rice when chicken has cooked one-half hour. For each serving, tear off a square of quilted broiling foil. Cup edges to hold ingredients. In each square mix:

½ cup packaged pre-cooked rice
½ cup water
2 - 3 tablespoons marinade

1 teaspoon butter
½ teaspoon salt

Bring corners and edges of quilted foil together; twist to seal. Place packets of rice on coals, twisted sides up, about 10 minutes before chicken is done. ⇘ To serve twist open rice packets and place in center of heated serving plate. Surround with chicken. Chicken will be crispy and flame colored; rice will match in color and flavor.

3 OR 4 SERVINGS

Cinnamon Chick

1 frying chicken, cut into serving
  pieces
½ cup dry sherry wine
6 tablespoons honey

2 teaspoons ground cinnamon
1 teaspoon curry powder
1 teaspoon garlic salt
  Quilted broiling foil

Wash chicken and dry each piece with paper toweling. Place pieces in a shallow dish or pan. ε In a small bowl, combine the sherry, honey and seasonings. Pour over chicken. Marinate for at least 1 hour, turning chicken occasionally. ε Line firebox with quilted broiling foil. When fire has burned to gray coals, place pieces of chicken on grill, not too close to the heat. Reserve remainder of the marinade. Cook 10 to 12 minutes on each side, or until golden brown. Baste often with the marinade. When chicken is thoroughly done, remove to warm serving platter. Garnish, if desired, with spiced kumquats and green-tinted pear halves.

4 SERVINGS

Chicken Livers with Colbert Sauce

12 chicken livers
Salt and pepper
12 slices bacon
⅔ cup melted butter
1 cup bread crumbs

1 cup bouillon
Juice of 1 lemon
¼ cup grated nutmeg
2 tablespoons sherry
¼ cup parsley, chopped

Line firebox of grill with foil, add charcoal, light, and let burn until flames die and gray ashes appear. ❧ Cut chicken livers into 1-inch squares, as nearly as possible, and divide into 4 portions. Season with salt and pepper and run them onto 4 skewers, alternating each piece with a piece of bacon, also cut in squares. Coat each with melted butter, roll in bread crumbs, and broil 10 to 12 minutes. ❧ Slide liver and bacon from skewers onto hot plates and pour Colbert Sauce over each. Serve with a border of saffron rice. A compote of cherries or boysenberries sprinkled with Cointreau makes an excellent accompaniment.

COLBERT SAUCE: Bring bouillon to a boil in saucepan, remove from fire and add 3½ ounces of the butter, beating with an egg beater until thoroughly mixed. Add lemon juice, nutmeg, and sherry. Strain and add chopped parsley.

4 SERVINGS

Rock Cornish Hen Italian

6 Italian sausages
12 green onions, sliced
2 cloves garlic, finely chopped
¼ cup butter
1 7½-ounce can pitted ripe olives
12 fresh mushrooms, thinly sliced

½ teaspoon salt
Dash pepper
6 tablespoons olive oil
1 teaspoon basil
6 Rock Cornish hens
6 teaspoons butter
Quilted broiling foil

Cook sausages over low heat in small amount of water, for 15 minutes. Drain, cool, remove skins and cut into thin slices. ࢤ Cook onions and garlic in butter until soft but not brown. Drain olives and reserve 6 for garnish; cut remainder into thin slices. ࢤ Combine sausage slices, onions, garlic, olives, mushrooms, salt and pepper, 2 tablespoons olive oil, ¾ teaspoon basil. Mix thoroughly. ࢤ Place 1 teaspoon soft butter in cavity of each bird; stuff with sausage mixture. Close openings with toothpicks or little skewers and truss with soft cord. Brush skins with remaining oil and basil. Place 3 olive slices along breastbone of each bird. ࢤ Cut 6 squares of quilted broiling foil. Place 1 bird in middle of each; wrap tightly, folding edges to seal. ࢤ Line firebox with quilted broiling foil. When coals have burned down to gray ash, cook Rock Cornish hens in foil over hot coals on grill for 1½ hours, turning every 15 minutes. ࢤ Serve in foil boats to retain natural juices.

6 SERVINGS

Grilled Stuffed Turkey

1 10- to 12-pound oven-ready turkey

STUFFING:

½ cup soy sauce
½ cup melted butter
½ cup water
½ cup sherry wine
 2 quarts croutons
 1 cup finely chopped onion
½ teaspoon ground sage
½ teaspoon poultry seasoning
 1 teaspoon salt
½ teaspoon pepper

BASTING SAUCE:

½ cup soy sauce
⅓ cup olive or corn oil
 1 teaspoon thyme
 1 teaspoon celery salt
 1 teaspoon salt
½ teaspoon pepper
¼ teaspoon monosodium glutamate
¼ cup white wine
¼ cup brandy
   Quilted broiling foil

Liberally rub cavity and outside of turkey with soy sauce. Combine remaining ingredients and mix lightly but thoroughly. Stuff loosely into cavity of turkey. Close openings with skewers, truss wings over back and tie legs together with heavy cord. Place breast up on large square of quilted broiling foil. ❧ Combine all ingredients of basting sauce and brush entire outer surface of turkey; then wrap foil around it. Pour ½ cup of basting sauce over fowl just before finally closing the wrapping. ❧ Place on grill away from fire, using indirect heat. Close hood and grill for 2½ hours at moderate temperature. Unfold foil, baste liberally and continue grilling at slightly lower heat for about 3 hours, using heavy smoke on charcoal. (Use water-soaked hickory chips on green wood.) ❧ Continue to grill, basting occasionally, until the turkey is a deep golden color and tests done. Let stand about ½ hour for easier carving.

10 TO 12 SERVINGS

Turkey on a Spit APRICOT-RICE STUFFING

6-pound junior turkey

APRICOT-RICE STUFFING:
1 cup raw white rice
1 cup dried apricots
½ cup butter
1½ cups onion, finely chopped
2 cups celery, finely chopped

½ teaspoon salt
½ teaspoon pepper
½ teaspoon poultry seasoning

APRICOT GLAZE:
½ cup apricot nectar
¼ cup lemon juice
½ cup honey

Wash turkey well inside and out, drying thoroughly with paper towels. Cook rice according to package directions. Meanwhile pour boiling water over apricots, let stand 5 minutes, drain, and chop fine. In large skillet melt butter and cook onion and celery until golden. Add seasonings, apricots, and cooked rice, tossing with fork until blended. Stuff neck and body cavities of turkey about three-fourths full. Truss bird, folding wings and skewering close to body. Tie legs together tightly, bringing cord under tail and over breast. Insert spit rod through center of body cavity, balancing carefully. Tighten skewer at each end to hold turkey securely. Insert meat thermometer in center of inner thigh muscle, not touching bone. ষ Line firebox with quilted foil, add charcoal and light. Let coals burn until gray ashes cover the coals and flames subside. Place spit about 8 inches over coals, making sure that spit turns in front of coals and that drip pan is in place under bird. Roast turkey 10 minutes, then brush with Apricot Glaze every 20 minutes. Cook about 2 hours, or until meat thermometer reads 290° F.

6 SERVINGS

Hula Duck

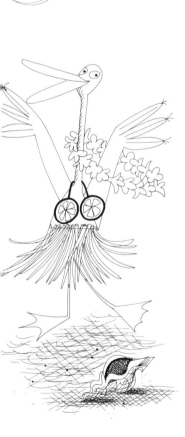

1 Long Island duckling
1 cup soy sauce
½ cup water
2 tablespoons cider vinegar
1 tablespoon lemon juice
1 teaspoon sugar
¼ teaspoon pepper

¼ teaspoon ground ginger
1 clove garlic, crushed
Dash Tabasco sauce

GARNISH:
2 bunches small green onions
2 round slices orange

Clean and dry duckling. Mix barbecue sauce ingredients, pour over duckling in bowl, and marinate about 4 hours, turning duck occasionally to cover with sauce. ❧ Build charcoal fire in grill with motor-driven spit and hood. Bank the coals at back of grill. It is necessary that the fire be kept *behind* the duck so that drippings can be caught in the broiler pan below the spit. This pan should be lined with a folded length of aluminum foil with the folded end extending up at the back so that drippings run down into the pan. ❧ When coals are completely red, place spitted duckling in position. Cook one hour, basting occasionally, then prick duck to allow fat to run out. Cook 1 to 1½ hours longer, basting now and then. If needed, add briquets to fire to maintain heat. ❧ When duck tests done (leg moves easily from body and skin is a deep bronze color), remove to warm platter to "dress." String green ends of onions using a darning needle and double thread to fashion a hula skirt. Use the 2 orange slices as costume top. ❧ If you like gravy with this duckling, slice the white part of the green onions into basting pan with 2 tablespoons flour. Blend well and brown, then add flour and water mixture to thicken.

2 OR 3 SERVINGS

NOTE: Ducklings vary in size. The larger ones have more fat, and are not as desirable as smaller ones, 3 to 4 pounds.

Orange Duck on a Spit

2 4½- to 5-pound ducks
4 oranges
½ cup olive oil
¼ cup Cointreau
½ teaspoon salt
¼ teaspoon freshly ground pepper
½ teaspoon basil

¼ teaspoon rosemary
½ teaspoon tarragon
¾ cup butter or margarine, melted
¾ cup orange juice
2 tablespoons grated orange rind
2 tablespoons chopped water cress
Quilted broiling foil

Line firebox with foil. Add briquets and light. Move burning briquets to back of grill; allow 30 minutes before cooking. For this recipe, you will need a motor-driven spit or barbecue rack. 🦢 Stuff ducks with orange pieces. Arrange and balance them on spit or rack, and attach to grill. Allow approximately 2 hours cooking time. 🦢 In a small bowl, combine oil, Cointreau and seasonings, basting ducks with this mixture every 10 to 15 minutes. (Place drip pan under ducks or fashion one out of foil.) 🦢 For Orange-Butter Sauce, combine melted butter, orange juice, orange rind and water cress; simmer for 15 minutes, stirring occasionally. Keep warm on back of grill. 🦢 Remove ducks to large serving platter; garnish with orange slices and parsley or water cress. Serve with hot orange-butter sauce. If ducks can not be served at once, wrap each in foil and set at side of grill to keep warm.

6 SERVINGS

Simple Salmon

1 small salmon, 5 to 7 pounds	1 clove garlic, mashed
10 to 12 slices bacon	4 sprigs parsley
1 large white onion, sliced	6 strips lemon rind
1 green pepper, sliced	Capers (optional)
2 teaspoons salt	Quilted broiling foil
½ teaspoon pepper	

Line firebox of grill with quilted broiling foil. Add charcoal, light and let burn until gray ash covers coals. ❧ Rub fish inside and outside with salt and pepper and inside only with garlic. Combine all remaining ingredients except 2 slices of bacon and stuff salmon. Place a strip of bacon on each side of fish and wrap in quilted broiling foil. Tie foil to fish securely from end to end with cord or fine wire. Grill about 6 inches over medium coals for from ½ to 1½ hours, or until flesh flakes easily. Turn every ½ hour during cooking. ❧ Delightful served with tartar sauce, lemon wedges, mashed potatoes or buttered new potatoes, and spinach.

10 TO 12 SERVINGS

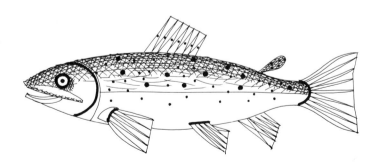

Salmon Steaks Stroganoff

4 1-inch thick salmon steaks
1 tablespoon lemon juice
1 tablespoon melted butter
1 teaspoon salt
½ teaspoon black pepper
1 teaspoon sweet basil

½ teaspoon onion salt
½ teaspoon rosemary
½ teaspoon paprika
2 cups sour cream
Quilted broiling foil

Line firebox of grill with quilted broiling foil. Add charcoal, light and let burn until flames have subsided. ✃ Brush salmon steaks on both sides with lemon juice. Cut 4 strips of quilted foil 3 times the width and 1½ times the length of the steaks. Brush steaks with butter and place on one-half of individual foil strip. Place on grill and brown lightly on each side. Remove from grill. ✃ Mix basil, onion salt, rosemary and paprika. Spoon one-fourth of sour cream on each steak. Sprinkle with one-fourth of herb mixture. Fold foil over each steak, then triple-fold edges together to seal. ✃ Return packets to grill. Cook for 5 to 7 minutes, turning frequently. Place on plates and cross-slash packets, folding back flaps to open.

4 SERVINGS

Chag Ha Sesame Salmon

4 center-cut salmon steaks
4 eggs
 Salt
 Pepper
 Monosodium glutamate

Sesame seeds
1 small jar sweet pickles and
 pickle liquid
Melted butter
Quilted broiling foil

Beat eggs lightly, add salt, pepper, and monosodium glutamate. Dip salmon steak into egg mixture and press into sesame seeds until completely covered. Sprinkle steaks generously with liquid from pickles, and arrange each on a sheet of foil. Fold loosely to cover. ❧ Broil 15 minutes on each side, or until salmon tests flaky. Just before steaks are completely cooked, carefully remove foil and let them brown over coals. ❧ Arrange salmon steaks on warm platter, drizzle about a teaspoon of melted butter over each, and garnish with lemon slices, sweet pickle slices, and parsley.

4 SERVINGS

Guamanian Tuna Steak

4 pieces fresh tuna, about 5 inches in
    diameter and ¾ inch thick
½ cup melted butter
  1 tablespoon lemon juice
  1 tablespoon parsley, chopped
  1 teaspoon salt

¼ teaspoon cayenne
  1 tablespoon onion, minced
  1 clove garlic, minced
¼ teaspoon nutmeg
¼ teaspoon cloves

Blend all sauce ingredients thoroughly and brush on both sides of tuna steaks. Grill steaks over hot charcoal, turning and brushing with sauce every 5 minutes. Allow 20 minutes cooking time, or until fish tastes flaky. ❧ Serve tuna on palm leaves and garnish with shredded coconut.

4 SERVINGS

Aloha Barbecued Swordfish

6 swordfish steaks
½ teaspoon fennel seed
½ cup lemon juice
¾ cup salad oil

Few drops Tabasco sauce
Pimiento-stuffed olives
Quilted broiling foil

Mix fennel seed, lemon juice, oil and Tabasco sauce. Brush onto swordfish or, better still, let fish soak in this marinade for 30 minutes. (If frozen swordfish is used, defrost ahead of time in refrigerator until just-thawed.) Wrap each steak in large squares of quilted foil; double seal top and ends by folding edges over each other several times. Place on rack over hot coals. Cook for 30 minutes, turning after 15 minutes of cooking. Open foil packages carefully to save all the juices. Slide fish onto warm plates and pour juices over them. Garnish with stuffed olives. Dash tops of swordfish with paprika if they have not colored enough to suit you.

6 SERVINGS

NOTE: You will also find this fish delicious if you brown it first on grill for a few minutes, brushing with marinade, then wrap in foil to finish cooking.

Whitefish Supreme

1 fresh whitefish, filleted
   (fresh lake trout may be used)
¼ pound butter or margarine
½ teaspoon sweet basil, marjoram
   and tarragon, combined

1 teaspoon Worcestershire sauce
1 tablespoon lemon juice
1 medium Bermuda onion
   Quilted broiling foil

Line firebox of grill with quilted foil. Place charcoal in firebox; ignite and let burn until coals are covered with gray ashes. Knock off ashes and spread coals for even distribution of heat. Meanwhile, in small pan, melt butter and add herbs, Worcestershire sauce and lemon juice. Blend well and set aside on back of grill to keep warm and absorb flavor. Slice onion and separate into rings. ♥ Line one side only of a long-handled hinged wire broiler with quilted foil. Lay filets on foil, skin side down. Close broiler and hold it with skin side very close to coals. Sear quickly so that skin sticks to broiler and will separate from fish. Remove broiler from heat. Open it and pull skin free with the help of a spatula. It's really quite simple to do. Discard foil and skin. Cover both sides of filets with onion rings. Drizzle with some of the butter sauce. Close broiler and place over coals. Grill fish 12 to 15 minutes, turning broiler several times and brushing fish with butter sauce each time. ♥ Turn fish carefully onto warm platter. Season lightly with salt and pepper. Garnish with sliced tomatoes and fresh parsley.

4 SERVINGS

NOTE: This is a delicious and unusual treatment for this delicate fish. If you don't want to bother with removing the skin, simply place filets in hinged broiler. Cover with onion rings and brush with the herbed butter sauce. Grill until browned and tender, about 15 minutes. Brush and turn frequently.

Barbecued Trout

6 medium-size dressed trout
Salt
⅓ cup sherry
⅓ cup melted butter
2 tablespoons lemon juice
6 slices bacon

SAUCE:
2 teaspoons sesame seeds
¼ cup butter
1 tablespoon sherry
1 tablespoon lemon juice

Sprinkle trout cavity with salt. Combine sherry, butter, and lemon juice and pour over trout to marinate for 1 hour, turning once after 30 minutes. Remove trout and wrap each with strip of bacon. ❧ Cook trout over medium-hot coals until bacon is crisp, basting 3 or 4 times with remaining marinade. Turn only once. ❧ While trout is cooking, brown sesame seeds in butter, add sherry and lemon juice. Serve hot over trout.

6 SERVINGS

Trout en Papillote

1 fresh or frozen trout
4 tablespoons clam juice
1 ½ tablespoons minced clams
1 ½ tablespoons minced mushrooms
½ teaspoon curry powder
¼ teaspoon monosodium glutamate
Melted butter
Diced crisp bacon
Vinegar-wilted water cress
Quilted broiling foil

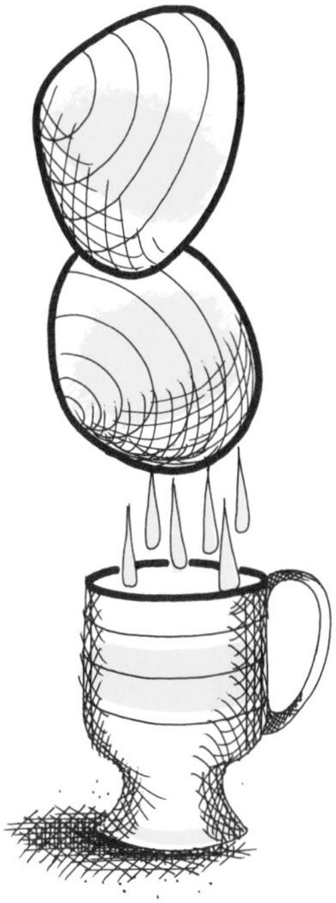

Line brazier with quilted broiling foil. Add charcoal, light and burn until flames die down. ❧ Do not remove head or tail from fish. Brush liberally with clam juice, inside and out. Combine clams, mushrooms, curry powder and monosodium glutamate, moisten with clam juice. Stuff fish and again brush with clam juice. ❧ Cut a piece of 14-inch quilted foil the length and twice the width of the trout, plus a margin of 1 ½ inches all around. Oil lightly. ❧ Place fish on half of piece of foil, fold other half over fish. Starting at one end, make overlapping folds, sealing edge of foil securely. ❧ Cook over hot coals 2 minutes; turn and cook 2 minutes. Repeat, cooking trout a total of 4 minutes per side. ❧ Serve trout in quilted foil papillote on a bed of diced bacon and vinegar-wilted water cress. Let the consumer slash open the papillote.

1 SERVING

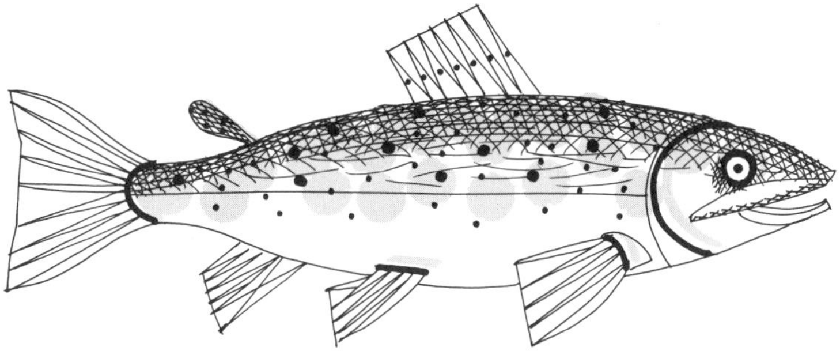

Barbecued Seafood Shibusa

KABOB ITEMS:

12 scallops
12 green shrimp
12 pieces lobster meat, cut to
    correspond in size with scallops
12 whole small tomatoes
12 mushrooms
12 pieces green pepper
36 strips bacon

MARINADE:

2 cups olive oil
¾ cup soy sauce
¼ cup Worcestershire sauce
½ cup lemon juice
½ cup wine vinegar
1 cup Chablis wine
2 tablespoons brown sugar
1 tablespoon coarse ground pepper
2 teaspoons dried parsley flakes
2 teaspoons Mei Yen powder
3 teaspoons orange peel

Marinate the seafood and vegetables for about 2 hours in marinade prior to barbecuing. ❧ Use foil for liner of firebox grill. Add charcoal and light. A very hot fire is best for these kabobs. ❧ Wrap each piece of seafood in a bacon strip and alternately thread 2 pieces of each item on six skewers. Allow approximately 10 minutes of grilling for each side. Brush kabobs with marinade during the last 5 minutes of barbecuing. If hand skewers are used it is necessary to keep rotating them. ❧ Slide kabobs off skewers and serve with ginger sprouts and rice.

6 SERVINGS

Oyster-Shrimp Kabobs

2 pounds uncooked shrimp
1 pound sliced bacon
1 quart oysters
8 skewers; kabob rack
   Quilted broiling foil

DIP MIXTURES FOR OYSTERS:

¾ cup yellow corn meal
  4 tablespoons curry powder
¾ cup yellow corn meal
  4 tablespoons Parmesan cheese

Line brazier with quilted broiling foil. Add charcoal, light and let burn until flames have subsided. ≥ Peel and de-vein shrimp. Cut bacon slices in thirds. Tear off 2 squares of 14-inch broiling foil. Mix corn meal and curry powder on one; corn meal and Parmesan cheese on the other. ≥ Dip half the oysters in corn-meal-and-curry mix. Wrap each with bacon strip. Dip remaining half of oysters in corn-meal-and-cheese mix and wrap each with bacon strip. ≥ Thread alternately on skewers: shrimp, corn-meal-curry-dipped oyster, then corn-meal-cheese-dipped oyster. Repeat. Allow space on either end of skewers to fit into notches of kabob rack. Place skewers in position. ≥ Place kabob rack over hot charcoal. Turn skewers frequently to assure even cooking. When oysters are golden brown, remove skewers and serve.

8 SERVINGS

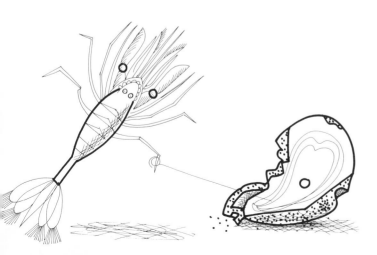

Sizzling Lobsters Supreme

4 live 1½-pound Maine lobsters
Monosodium glutamate
1 pound butter
2 cloves garlic
4 teaspoons salt
½ teaspoon freshly ground coarse
pepper

½ cup fresh parsley, chopped
3 tablespoons minced chives
1 teaspoon dried tarragon
⅔ cup fresh lemon juice
Wedges of lemon

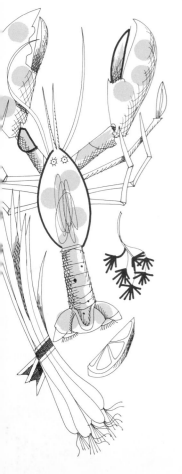

Line outdoor grill with quilted foil. Heap with briquets and light. Let fire burn about 30 minutes, or until gray ashes cover briquets. ᔢ *To prepare lobsters:* Place lobster on its back and sever spinal cord by inserting a sharp knife between body shell and tail segment. Now split it by pulling a sharp heavy knife lengthwise from head to tail right through its heavy shell. Remove the stomach, just back of the head, and the intestinal vein running from the stomach to the tip of the tail. Leave in the grayish-looking liver. Crack the claws. Sprinkle flesh with a little monosodium glutamate. ᔢ Melt butter and add mashed garlic, 1 teaspoon monosodium glutamate and the rest of the ingredients except lemon wedges. Roll lobsters in sauce; then place on grill flesh side down about 3 inches from coals. Cook until meat becomes a delicate brown, 12 to 15 minutes. Keep butter sauce warm. ᔢ Remove lobsters to wooden plank or individual platters. Ladle more butter sauce on top. Garnish with lemon wedges. Pass the extra sauce to guests for dunking.

4 SERVINGS

NOTE: If Maine lobsters are not available, they can be shipped live by either rail or air express. Whole lobsters cooked in the shell (either Eastern or the Western spiny type), and also fresh and frozen lobster tails are available almost everywhere. They may be used for this recipe. Split and broil, brushing with the butter sauce. Cook briefly, since they're already cooked.

Lobster Broil Japanese

4 Pacific or spiny lobsters
8 dried mushrooms (shitake, if
   available)
8 green onions
¼ cup soy sauce
2 tablespoons sake wine
2 tablespoons sugar

2 tablespoons finely cut ginger
Few grains sansho powder
   (Japanese pepper), or use
   cayenne
¼ cup lime skin, finely cut
8 slices of lime, quartered
Quilted broiling foil

Soak dried mushrooms in water for 30 minutes. ॐ Line firebox of grill with quilted foil, add charcoal, light, and let burn until gray ashes cover coals and flames have become quiet. ॐ Split lobsters in two, lengthwise. ॐ In large bowl mix soy sauce, sake, sugar, ginger, sansho or cayenne, and lime skin. Cut green onions 2 inches long and shred lengthwise. ॐ Place lobsters and mushrooms on grill, brush with the sauce 3 times during 20-minute cooking period. Put mushrooms on lobster, 1 on each piece, and grill for 5 minutes. ॐ Just before serving put a shredded green onion under each mushroom, and anchor a quartered lime on top of each, using small skewers.

4 SERVINGS

Kulani Champagne Lobster

6 frozen rock-lobster tails
   (about 8 ounces each) thawed
¼ cup butter
1 small white onion, sliced
3 tablespoons flour
1 10½-ounce can consommé
½ teaspoon salt
   Dash of white pepper

1 cup California champagne
4 whole cloves
2 teaspoons peppercorns
1 teaspoon sugar
2 tablespoons lemon juice
½ cup orange juice
   Quilted broiling foil

Line firebox of grill with foil. Let fire burn down to gray ash before cooking, about 30 minutes. ৶ To prepare Brown Sauce: melt butter in aluminum pan. Sauté onion until soft; remove and discard. Add flour and cook, stirring constantly, until smooth and brown. Add consommé gradually and cook over low heat, stirring until thickened, 5 to 6 minutes. Add salt and pepper. Remove from heat and set aside. ৶ To prepare Champagne Sauce: combine champagne, cloves and peppercorns in a foil pan. Cook over low heat for about 10 minutes. Add the brown sauce, sugar, lemon juice and orange juice. Simmer for 10 minutes. Strain and set aside. May be made ahead and refrigerated. ৶ Cut along membrane of completely thawed lobster and rip open. Remove lobster meat and marinate in champagne sauce for 30 minutes. ৶ Tear off six 14-inch strips of quilted broiling foil. Make each into a packet by folding edges of 3 sides over several times to seal. Insert one lobster tail and 6 tablespoons champagne sauce into each packet. Fold remaining edge several times to seal. Reserve remaining sauce to serve with cooked lobster. ৶ Place packets on grill and cook for 30 to 40 minutes, turning every 5 minutes. ৶ Remove from fire. Make a criss-cross slash in each packet and serve with extra champagne sauce.

6 SERVINGS

Broiled Lobster Tails Mediterranean

12 lobster tails (in shells)
1 cup dry white wine
½ cup olive oil
¼ cup fresh lemon juice
1 teaspoon salt

¼ teaspoon cayenne pepper
1 clove pressed garlic
½ cup grated Parmesan cheese
Quilted broiling foil

Line firebox of grill with quilted foil. Let coals burn down until covered with a gray ash. ᨞ In a 1½-quart bowl, combine wine, olive oil, lemon juice, salt, cayenne pepper and garlic. Slit the lobster tails along the full length of the membrane. Remove membrane; spread open and remove intestinal vein. ᨞ Brush meat thoroughly with marinating mixture. Place shell side down on the grill, 2 inches over the coals; broil 6 to 8 minutes. Brush each tail again with the mixture, turn and broil 6 minutes more. Turn meat side up and sprinkle 1 teaspoon cheese over each lobster tail. When cheese has melted, remove to warm platter. Serve with lemon wedges and hot garlic bread.

6 SERVINGS

Far Eastern Charcoal-Broiled Shrimp

1½ pounds raw shrimp (10 to 12 per pound)
3 tablespoons soy sauce
1 teaspoon grated fresh ginger
1 teaspoon onion juice
1 tablespoon minced fresh tarragon

3 drops Tabasco sauce
⅓ cup soy oil
4 slices bacon, ¼ inch thick
1 small can water chestnuts
Quilted broiling foil

Shell and de-vein shrimp; rinse and pat dry. Place in shallow pan. Combine soy sauce, ginger, onion juice, tarragon and Tabasco; pour over shrimp. Marinate 15 minutes, turning shrimp several times. Add soy oil and marinate 30 minutes longer. ❧ Line firebox with foil. While fire is burning down, cook bacon until soft but not browned; cut into 2-inch strips. ❧ Fold each shrimp over a square of bacon and thread on metal skewers alternately with water chestnuts. (A cork placed on the end of each skewer prevents food from slipping off.) Place skewers in marinade while preparing Chinese Pea Pods in Foil. ❧ Grill for about 10 minutes, turning and basting with marinade frequently. Serve on bed of hot Chinese Pea Pods.

CHINESE PEA PODS IN FOIL:
1 pound fresh (or 2 8-ounce packages frozen) Chinese pea pods
2 tablespoons soy oil

1 teaspoon onion powder
½ teaspoon salt
Dash monosodium glutamate

Wash and string pea pods; place in quilted aluminum foil pan. Add soy oil, onion powder, salt and monosodium glutamate. Stir until pea pods are well coated. Wrap pan tightly in foil. Cook on grill for 15 minutes, turning package upside down several times. Drain off excess oil and serve on heated platter, topped with Charcoal Broiled Shrimp.

4 SERVINGS

Shrimp on the Rocks

2½ pounds raw shrimp (medium size)
⅔ cup melted butter
1 ounce sherry
½ cup parsley, chopped
3 tablespoons green pepper, chopped
1 teaspoon salt
½ teaspoon fresh milled black pepper
1 tablespoon monosodium glutamate
Quilted broiling foil

Peel and de-vein shrimp. Mix other ingredients. Divide shrimp into 6 equal portions, and place each in center of a 10-inch strip of quilted foil. Pour the butter and seasoning mix equally over each. Fold edges of foil together to form an air-tight envelope. ‎ Line firebox with quilted foil, add briquets and light. Allow fire to burn down to a moderately hot bed of glowing coals. No grill is used, as the shrimp are cooked directly on glowing briquets. Cook for a total of 8 minutes, turning once. 2 or 3 peeled garlic buds tossed directly into fire for last 5 minutes of cooking act as an appetite stimulator. ‎ To serve, fold back foil from top of shrimp and garnish with parsley and lemon quarters. Macaroni salad, sliced tomatoes, and hot garlic bread are good accompaniments.

6 SERVINGS

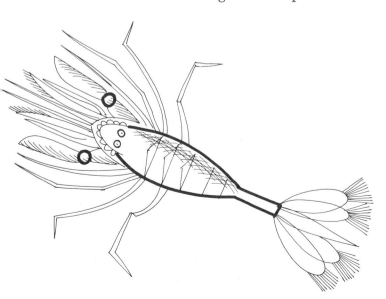

Old-Fashioned Clambake

4 dozen round clams
5 broiling chickens
10 pounds bluefish
10 pounds potatoes
4 dozen ears corn
20 small live lobsters
1 pound butter, melted

OPTIONAL:
20 tomatoes
1 bushel steaming clams, to be
   served before bake is done

STUFFING FOR CLAMS (OPTIONAL):
2 loaves stale bread, toasted and
   broken into bits
2 eggs
1 onion, chopped fine
Salt (very little)
Pepper
Poultry seasoning to taste
1½ cups water

Select a large spot of bare ground for bake, above tide level if on the beach. Arrange large, round stones about 1 foot in diameter to cover a circle about 5 feet in diameter and 1½ feet high. Build a very hot fire of wood on the stones, and let burn for about 2 hours. Meanwhile prepare food. Have it *all* ready, as quick work is necessary when putting it on. ᧧ Stuff the clam shells (if desired) with the above mixture, putting clam in on top of stuffing. Cut chickens in quarters, and wrap in cheesecloth, or very loosely in broiling foil. Cut fish in portions and also wrap. Wash potatoes, and husk corn, leaving last 4 husks on. If you have wire mesh baskets, or, better still, unpainted wire dish drainers, place all items of same food in a separate basket. If not, wrap same food items in cheesecloth, or place on individual trays from which you can slide the food quickly. ᧧ When a drop of water spits back quickly from the hot stones they are ready. Have canvas nearby. Rake off any unburned wood, and quickly throw on seaweed, spreading it over all the rocks to a depth of about 6 inches. If no seaweed is available, use clean burlap bags, wet in salt water. Immediately place on seaweed the baskets of food, or slide off the trays evenly around, keeping each item in a place by itself. Cover with more seaweed and at once cover the whole with canvas, weighting down with stones. Put a potato under the canvas. When it is done, about 2 hours, the bake is ready. Serve with melted butter, salt, pepper, and catsup.

20 SERVINGS

Montana Venison Steak

8 6-ounce venison steaks, 1 inch thick
1½ teaspoons unseasoned meat tenderizer
⅔ cup olive oil
⅓ cup salad oil
¼ cup wine vinegar
¼ cup lemon juice
1 teaspoon salt
¼ teaspoon pepper
1 teaspoon sugar
½ teaspoon dried thyme leaves
1 cup parsley, finely chopped
2 cloves garlic, finely chopped
1 large onion, thinly sliced
4 loaves French bread (½ pound size)
Quilted broiling foil

Bring steak to room temperature and place in shallow dish. Sprinkle both sides evenly with meat tenderizer. Combine other ingredients, except onion, in covered jar and shake well. Pour over steak and marinate 1 hour. ঙ Start fire and adjust grill so that it is 4 inches from coals. About 15 minutes before grilling venison, wrap bread loaves individually in foil and place on grill until red hot (about 20 minutes). Grill venison 3 minutes on each side for medium rare. ঙ Cut bread loaves in half lengthwise, arrange 2 steaks on bottom half of each, cover with onions, and top with upper half of loaf. Crush foil around bread and cut loaves in half crosswise to serve.

8 SERVINGS

NOTE: If venison is from young deer no tenderizer is necessary.

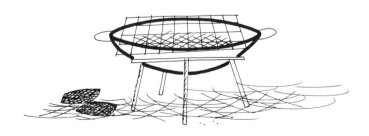

Roast Venison Trailstyle

2½-pound venison roast
3 slices bacon
1 tablespoon horse-radish
3 tablespoons sherry wine

MARINADE:
1 medium onion, sliced
1 cup salad oil
½ cup lemon juice
1 teaspoon salt

The day before the cookout, combine marinade ingredients in large bowl, immerse meat, cover tightly and place in refrigerator. ᓓ About 2 hours before serving time, set up grill with spit attached. Line firebox with quilted broiling foil, add charcoal and let burn 45 minutes, or until gray ashes are formed over charcoal. Put spit through roast, wrap bacon around it, and truss firmly to the spit. While roast is cooking continue to baste with marinade. When roast is done (about 1 hour), remove from spit and stir horse-radish and sherry into remaining marinade to serve over it.

4 SERVINGS

NOTE: As most connoisseurs prefer their venison rare, and cuts and age of meat vary greatly, it is wise to test the meat at the end of 40 minutes or so.

Colorado Hunting Camp Elk Steak

Elk steak, 2 to 2½ inches thick
¼ teaspoon pepper
¼ teaspoon salt
½ teaspoon chili powder

¼ teaspoon garlic salt
¼ teaspoon celery salt
½ teaspoon onion salt
Quilted broiling foil

Prepare and cool meat at least 24 hours before cutting into steaks. Wipe meat clean with damp cloth and sprinkle evenly on all sides with the above spices. Let stand at room temperature 45 minutes while preparing sauce in large skillet.

SAUCE:
1 15-ounce can tomato sauce
½ pint water
4 tablespoons olive or salad oil
¼ cup pineapple or peach juice
1 teaspoon onion salt
1 teaspoon garlic salt

2 teaspoons vinegar or lemon juice
1 teaspoon celery salt
1 teaspoon chili powder
½ teaspoon pepper
½ teaspoon salt
½ cup brown sugar
1 tablespoon Worcestershire sauce

Mix all ingredients and simmer over a low fire. ⮞ Make sure charcoal is low and evenly distributed. Broil meat for 20 minutes, or until lightly brown, on each side. Then wrap in quilted broiling foil and broil for 45 minutes to 1 hour. At 15-minute intervals turn, open foil, and baste meat heavily with sauce. Reserve remaining sauce to serve over meat. ⮞ To complete this meal, wash several carrots and potatoes with a stiff brush, wrap each in quilted foil and bake directly over coals, turning several times for 1 hour or until tender. Unwrap and add salt and butter.

NOTE: A similar beef steak may be substituted for the elk steak by the patio cooks. The number of servings depends on size of steak and appetites.

Kabobs

1 pound sirloin or top round steak,
    1 inch thick
1 pound veal steak, ½ inch thick
1 pound pork steak, ½ inch thick
2 large green peppers, cut into
    2-inch squares
4 medium onions, parboiled
    5 minutes, cut into quarters
4 baking apples, cut lengthwise
    into 6 wedges

MARINADE SAUCE:
  ½ cup salad oil
  ¼ cup soy sauce
  ½ cup dry red wine
1½ teaspoons ground ginger
  1 to 2 cloves garlic, finely chopped
  2 teaspoons curry powder
  2 tablespoons catsup
  ¼ teaspoon pepper
  ½ teaspoon Tabasco sauce

Measure marinade sauce ingredients into deep mixing bowl or jar of blender. Beat with electric or hand mixer or in blender until sauce is smooth and completely homogenized. ❧ Cut meat into 2-inch squares, place in refrigerator dish and add marinade sauce, making sure each piece is properly covered. Cover bowl and refrigerate from 12 to 36 hours, depending upon pungency of flavor desired. Mix several times during marinating period. ❧ Line charcoal grill with quilted foil, fill with charcoal and light. Unless the broiler is provided with an automatic rotator, the kabobs should be turned at frequent intervals by hand. ❧ When fire is moderately hot, remove meat from sauce. On large skewers alternate 3 pieces of meat with one of pepper, onion, or apple. Place apple next to pork, pepper next to veal, onion with beef. Mushroom caps may be placed on either end of the skewered meats. Brush vegetables and apple with marinade, then grill 25 to 30 minutes turning skewers frequently and basting several times during cooking. ❧ The kabob is most attractively served by removing it from the skewer and placing it in 2 rows on a preheated large platter which has been garnished with stuffed broiled tomatoes, green beans piquant, and deviled carrots. Flame the kabobs with pre-warmed brandy just before serving. Drink a fine red wine.

4 TO 6 SERVINGS

NOTE: A rice or cracked wheat pilaf would be good with this, too.

Scottish Mixed Grill FOR TWO HUNGRY PEOPLE

1 French lamb chop, 1¼ inches thick
1 kidney lamb chop, 1¼ inches thick
1 lamb kidney, split
4 thick slices bacon
1 slice calves' liver, ¾ inch thick
2 small sausages
2 potatoes, previously boiled, sliced
    ⅜ inch thick
1 tomato, halved
  Strips of red and green pepper,
    ¼ inch wide
  Parsley

CLAN GRAHAM BUTTER:

½ pound butter
¾ tablespoon lemon juice
½ tablespoon parsley, finely chopped
½ teaspoon salt
¼ teaspoon powdered thyme
⅛ teaspoon pepper

While fire is burning down to desired heat, brush lamb chops, kidney, and liver with Clan Graham Butter. Wrap bacon around kidney, fastening with small skewers. Place all on grill, cooking 15 to 25 minutes, depending on distance of grill from fire and desired degree of doneness. Brown sausages on grill, pricking skin with fork to prevent splitting. Place potato slices in foil pie pan with about ¼ of the Clan Graham Butter and fry 10 to 15 minutes. Brush halved tomato with the butter and grill 5 to 7 minutes. ❧ Arrange on 2 hot plates with one-half bacon-wrapped kidney, one-half liver slice, one-half tomato, and one chop on each. Brush all liberally with the butter, add potato slices equally. Garnish with strips of red and green pepper and parsley and serve immediately.

2 GENEROUS SERVINGS

Chicken Tamales en Grille

6 whole boned chicken breasts

FILLING:

6 ounces cooked ham, minced
1 small onion, chopped
Pinch fennel, chopped
¼ cup soft butter
¼ teaspoon paprika
1 teaspoon salt
Freshly ground pepper

¼ cup melted butter
¼ cup parsley, minced
12 pimiento halves
Toothpicks
Quilted broiling foil

Line firebox of grill with foil, add charcoal and light. Let burn until gray ashes cover coals and flames subside. ᏍᏌ Blend the filling ingredients to a paste consistency in a bowl. Place chicken breast on board and pound with wooden mallet until flat and the size of medium pancakes. Salt and pepper each piece. Spoon a small mound of ham mixture in center of each, roll, enclosing ends, and secure with toothpicks. Brush each tamale with melted butter and place on grill for about 4 minutes, turning to lightly brown all sides. ᏍᏌ Remove from grill and place each tamale on a foil square, 6 inches square, first removing toothpicks. Sprinkle with parsley and garnish with pimiento halves. Roll foil closed and twist ends. Return to grill for about 15 minutes on each side. ᏍᏌ At serving time let each guest unwrap his own tamale. Wild rice is a nice complement.

6 SERVINGS

Rabbit Royale

1 domestic rabbit, dressed and cut
    into serving pieces
Tabasco sauce

BASTING SAUCE:
1 teaspoon salt
1/4 teaspoon pepper
1/8 teaspoon each cinnamon, allspice,
    onion salt
1/2 teaspoon paprika
1/2 teaspoon pulverized dried
    mint leaves
1 tablespoon dried parsley
1/2 cup water
Juice of 1 lemon

Juice of 1 orange
1/2 cup butter
4 tablespoons kirsch
    or Oregon cherry brandy

FOR SERVING:
Sliced Italian bread
1 glass preserved cherries or
    cherry butter
Brandy

Sprinkle pieces of rabbit with Tabasco sauce and let stand while preparing basting sauce. Ș Blend all basting sauce ingredients except butter and brandy in saucepan. Simmer gently about 5 minutes and pour over rabbit. Let marinate while you make charcoal fire. Ș Line firebox of grill with quilted broiling foil. You may use some fiber glass filling to prevent flames if desired. Add charcoal and light. Let burn until coals are covered with gray ash and stop blazing. Ș Drain basting sauce from rabbit into small pan, add butter and brandy, simmer 2 or 3 minutes, and keep warm on back of grill. Baste rabbit pieces generously with sauce and grill, basting and turning often, until rabbit is very tender, about 1 hour. Never let the outside dry out, as it burns easily. Start grilling meaty side up. Ș To serve: Toast slices of Italian bread on grill, spread with preserved cherries, and give each slice a dash of brandy. The remaining basting sauce may be thickened and used for gravy.

4 SERVINGS

Lion's Head Chinese

2 pounds fresh pork, ground
1 6½-ounce can crabmeat, flaked
1 5-ounce can water chestnuts,
    minced
1 clove garlic, pressed
1 teaspoon grated onion
3 tablespoons soy sauce

3 tablespoons sherry wine
1 teaspoon brown sugar
½ teaspoon black pepper
¼ teaspoon ginger
2 eggs, lightly beaten
¼ cup flour

In large bowl combine all ingredients except eggs and flour. Mix thoroughly. Add eggs, then slowly mix in flour. Form into 4 large patties about 1 inch thick. This makes a soft, tender mixture. You may find it easier to grill the patties in a hinged-wire broiler so they can be turned without breaking or crumbling. ❧ Line firebox of grill with quilted foil before adding charcoal. Light fire and allow flames to subside and gray ashes to cover coals. Grill patties over coals until well done and browned, about 15 minutes on each side. ❧ This is nice served with rice, chopped spinach and wedges of fresh pineapple.

4 SERVINGS

Pakistani Barbecue Bread

BREAD:
1½ cups flour
1 egg yolk
⅓ cup water
½ teaspoon salt
3 ounces margarine

FOR GARNISH:
2 ripe tomatoes, sliced
4 leaves of lettuce

Quilted broiling foil

EGG MIXTURE:
3 large eggs
½ pound ground beef
1 medium onion, chopped
1 clove garlic, finely chopped
2 green onions, chopped
3 ounces mushrooms, sliced
½ pound fresh bean sprouts,
    or 1 can, drained
1½ teaspoons curry powder
¼ teaspoon pepper
1 teaspoon salt

To make the bread, mix, stir, and knead flour, egg yolk, water, and salt to make a homogeneous dough. Divide into 4 pieces. Shape each piece into a ball and roll out on a floured pastry-board to ⅛-inch thickness and circular in shape. Grease the upper half of the dough surface with margarine. Fold in two, making a half circle. Grease the upper half surface again with margarine, and again fold in two. The dough should now have the form of a quarter segment of a circle. Shape the dough again into a ball and repeat above procedure once more. For the last time, shape the dough into a ball and roll into a circular shape of ⅛-inch thickness. Set the 4 circles of dough aside. ❧ In a big bowl whip the 3 eggs for 2 minutes, then mix with the rest of the ingredients. Mix thoroughly! ❧ Cover the grill rack with 2 layers of quilted broiling foil. When well heated, grease the surface with margarine and grill the 4 pieces of dough until brown on one side. Turn over and cover the browned upper side with ¼ of the meat-egg mixture for each circle of dough. Grill until the other side of the dough is well browned and turn over. Grill until the egg mixture is set and brown. ❧ Serve on a plate with tomato slices and lettuce leaves artistically arranged. Parsley sprigs may be added for decoration.

2 GENEROUS SERVINGS

Crock Brats

12 Bratwurst sausages
1 bottle or can of beer

⅛ pound of butter

Soak 12 clear-skin Bratwurst sausages in water for 15 minutes. After soaking, place on grill with coals white hot. Roll half-turn approximately every 2 or 3 minutes. If coals begin to flame from drippings, put out with fine spray of water. Continue to roll sausages until evenly browned. ﾋ While sausages are cooking, place crock on grill with ⅛ pound butter and 1 bottle or can of beer. When sausages are cooked, place them in the crock. Place lid on, allowing sausages to steam in their own juice, beer and butter. ﾋ When everyone is seated the sausages may be served on potato buns and the last sausage will be as hot and juicy as the first. ﾋ Serve with coleslaw.

4 SERVINGS

Cranberry Dogs

2 pounds frankfurters (8 per
   pound)
1 1-pound can jellied cranberry
   sauce
½ cup sugar
1½ teaspoons curry powder
1 teaspoon ground cardamon

¼ teaspoon ground ginger
1 teaspoon salt
½ cup cider vinegar
2 tablespoons molasses
1½ teaspoons Worcestershire sauce
   Quilted broiling foil

In 2½-quart saucepan, combine all ingredients except frankfurters. Heat to boiling and simmer 5 minutes. Remove from heat and beat with rotary beater until thoroughly blended. ❧ Line firebox with quilted broiling foil. When coals are red hot, place Savory Baked Beans on grill. ❧ Make 3 diagonal cuts in frankfurters. Just before beans are ready to serve, place "dogs" on grill. Cook for about 7 minutes, frequently turning and basting with sauce. Serve hot.

SAVORY BAKED BEANS:

2 1-pound cans baked beans
1 medium onion, coarsely chopped
2 tablespoons salad oil

¼ cup molasses
½ cup catsup
½ teaspoon garlic salt

Sauté onions in oil until tender and golden. In 1-quart beanpot or casserole, combine all ingredients. Bake uncovered for about 1 hour on grill, or bake in oven at 350°F. for 30 minutes.

6 SERVINGS

South Seas Burgers

½ pound frozen shrimp
1½ pounds ground beef
1 egg
1 small can evaporated milk
1 4-ounce can mushrooms, stems and pieces
½ cup fine cracker crumbs

¼ cup finely diced onion
¼ cup finely diced green pepper
2 teaspoons curry powder
1½ teaspoons salt
Quilted broiling foil

GARNISH: onion rings, catsup

Shell and de-vein shrimp; chop into pieces. In large bowl, combine shrimp with beef, egg, milk, mushrooms, crumbs, onion, green pepper, curry and salt. Mix until well blended. Cover with quilted foil and let stand while preparing fire. Line charcoal grill with quilted broiling foil. Add charcoal, light and let burn until flames have died down. Form South Seas Burger mixture into 6 to 8 patties. Cook over coals about 9 minutes. Lift patties to individual squares of quilted foil. Replace on grill and cook for about 7 to 8 minutes. Serve on quilted foil squares, topping each patty with onion rings and catsup.

6 SERVINGS

Broiled Garland Stew

½ pound veal
½ pound beef, round steak or chuck
¼ pound salt pork
12 lamb kidneys
½ cup olive oil
 1 tablespoon lime or lemon juice
 1 tablespoon soy sauce

½ teaspoon salt
½ teaspoon coarse ground pepper
 3 cloves garlic, sliced
 3 medium-size tomatoes
 2 medium-size green peppers
  Quilted broiling foil

Cut meat into 1-inch cubes. Split kidneys and remove white membrane. (One-half pound veal or beef kidney, cut in cubes, may be used.) ৪ু With large needle and string, thread 4 individual portions of cubes of veal, beef, salt pork and kidneys alternately. Tie ends of string together, forming garlands about 5 inches in diameter. ৪ু Cut off a 3-foot length of quilted broiling foil. Fold in half, then triple-fold ½ inch along both sides, pressing and creasing to make a tight seal. Slip garlands of meat into open end of packet. Combine and pour over meat: olive oil, lime juice, soy sauce, salt, pepper and garlic. Fold open end of packet up so marinade will not seep out. Let stand at least 3 hours, or preferably overnight in the refrigerator. ৪ু Just before cooking time, quarter tomatoes, cut peppers into medium-size pieces and place in quilted foil packet with meat. Triple-fold end to seal. ৪ু Line firebox of brazier with quilted broiling foil. Add a heap of charcoal or briquets and light. Let burn down until there are no longer flames. Spread coals over area needed. ৪ু Place foil packet on grill about 3 inches above glowing coals. If packet is well sealed, it will puff up. Cook for about 15 minutes, then roll packet over. It will roll easily because of its inflated round shape. Too, the meat is automatically basted. The packet may deflate, but will puff up again. Cook about 15 minutes more. ৪ু Slit the foil packet crosswise and pull back the flaps. Lift out meat garlands and brown directly on grill for about 5 minutes. Meanwhile, let the sauce "cook down" in the packet. (Thickening may be added, if desired.) ৪ু Serve the individual portions with steamed rice. Cut and pull out strings. Spoon sauce over meat and rice. Garnish with slivers of ripe olives if desired.

4 SERVINGS